DATE DUE

Patterns of Protest

Patterns of Protest

Trajectories of Participation in Social Movements

Catherine Corrigall-Brown

Stanford University Press
Stanford, California

Stanford University Press
Stanford, California

Printed in the United States of America on acid-free, archival-quality paper

Library of Congress Cataloging-in-Publication Data
Corrigall-Brown, Catherine, author.
Patterns of protest : trajectories of participation in social movements / Catherine Corrigall-Brown.
     pages   cm
  Includes bibliographical references and index.
  ISBN 978-0-8047-7410-9 (alk. paper)
    1. Social movements—United States.   2. Political participation—United States.
3. Social action—United States.   4. Political activists—United States.   5. Social reformers—United States.   I. Title.
  HN57.C64 2012
  303.48'40973—dc22

                                                                      2011007293

Typeset by Motto Publishing Services in 10/14 Minion

For Steve

Contents

Illustrations

Figures

Tables

Acknowledgments

AS JOHN DONNE (ALMOST) FAMOUSLY SAID, "No woman is an island," and this could not be more apt in my case. In fact, there is nothing more sociological than recognizing that humans do not thrive in isolation from others. True to this, I am particularly fortunate to have received so much support from wonderful mentors, family, and friends that has allowed me to accomplish much more than I would have alone. Mentors such as David Snow, David Meyer, Edward Grabb, and Judith Stepan-Norris have encouraged and supported my work. Not only has their advice helped me develop this project from an idea into a book, but their assistance has proved invaluable in helping me develop as a scholar. In particular, the continued support of David Meyer and David Snow has been crucial as I navigate the choppy waters of academia. I greatly appreciate the time and energy they have dedicated to my scholarly development and their support of me and my work.

Many additional scholars agreed to read this book at various stages. Sidney Tarrow first suggested that I approach top scholars in the field to read the manuscript. After asking a group of academics whom I greatly admire to provide their comments, I was delighted that all of them agreed to read the book and gave me suggestions that were challenging and thoughtful. The willingness of these scholars to read and critique the work of a young academic with whom they had not previously worked is truly generous given the obviously intense demands on their time. I thank Holly McCammon, Suzanne Staggenborg, Sidney Tarrow, Doug McAdam, Bert Klandermans, Russell Dalton, David Meyer, and the anonymous reviewers from Stanford University Press for their time and energy. In particular I would also like to thank Holly for her support and encouragement of my overall professional development over long coffees at the meetings of the American Sociological Association. Her advice is always wise and provides a much-appreciated perspective. I also thank Russell Dalton for his suggestion of the Jennings data set and support through the Center for the Study of Democracy at the University of California–Irvine. I also acknowledge Hans-Dieter Klingemann for his encouragement of me and my work. While I may not have fully satisfied all of these scholars, this book is vastly improved because of their efforts.

Many colleagues have provided friendship and support that has made my academic life more enjoyable as I worked on this book. These include Steven Boutcher, Kelsy Kretschmer, Alix van Sickle, Ryan Acton, Rens Vliegenthart, and Sharon Oselin at the University of California–Irvine and Rima Wilkes, Edward Grabb, and Amy Lang at the University of British Columbia. In particular, I want to thank Rima Wilkes and Edward Grabb, both of whom read this manuscript too many times to count. Rima's frank appraisals and enthusiasm for my overall scholarly development helped support me during my time at the University of British Columbia. Ed's inspiring career, flair for language, and punctilious nature shaped me as a scholar and provided a wonderful sounding board for this work.

I also gratefully acknowledge the many granting agencies in Canada and the United States that have supported me and my research. The doctoral fellowship I received from the Social Sciences and Humanities Research Council of Canada as well as the support from the Center for the Study of Democracy at the University of California–Irvine has been invaluable. In addition, the Departments of Sociology at the University of California–Irvine and the University of British Columbia have provided enriching homes during the writing of this book.

I gratefully acknowledge M. Kent Jennings and colleagues, who collected a unique panel data set that provides the bases for Chapters 2 and 3. The efforts of scholars like Jennings and their willingness to share their data with others are critical to the academic enterprise.

I would also like to thank the activists whom I interviewed, who shared their stories with me. While they are not named, their lives and work form the backbone of this book. In a world filled with alienation and apathy, they have the courage to try to make a difference. Even though I do not agree with all of their views, their commitment to their beliefs and social change is an inspiration to me.

Kate Wahl, Executive Editor at Stanford University Press, has encouraged and supported this project since our first contact. Her enthusiasm and professionalism have eased the complicated process of publishing this book. I appreciate her belief in this project and her hard work in bringing the book to press. In addition, Joa Suorez did a great job organizing the reviews and back-cover material, Gretchen Otto and Carolyn Brown have been extremely helpful with the production process, Rob Ehle and Yvo Riezebos are responsible for the wonderful cover, and Christine Gever did an exceptional job copy-editing. Working with Stanford University Press has been a wonderful experience, from my initial contact with Kate through production.

Some people say that the apple does not fall far from the tree. I certainly hope that is the case for me. My parents, Melodie Corrigall and Hans Brown, are examples of the type of inspiring activists discussed in this book. They have worked their whole lives for causes they believe in and have not compromised in their efforts to create a more just and equitable world. It was they who first got me interested in social movements, when as a child I engaged in peace marches and picket lines with them. My father's enthusiasm and unwavering support and my mother's creativity and generosity have been my foundation.

My sister and best friend, Sarah, read and commented on this entire manuscript, reinforcing my belief that there is nothing at which she does not excel. I appreciate her encouragement, support, and wise advice, always. And to my brother-in-law, Neil, and my delightful nephew and good-luck charm, Barkley, thank you for the happy distractions throughout this process.

This book is dedicated to my husband, Steve. Since we met in the romantic setting of a political parties class, he has encouraged and believed in me and my work. Through an unending number of revisions, his support and love have been unwavering. I am forever grateful.

1 A Model of Participation

IF IT IS TRUE, AS AMOS OZ SAID, that "activism is a way of life," how do people come to embrace this lifestyle? Dorothy typifies one pathway to participation. She was born in Brooklyn, New York, and at the age of ten, she moved with her family to a tenement flat on Chicago's South Side when her father lost his job. After graduating from high school, she received a scholarship to attend the University of Illinois at Urbana-Champaign, where she became politically radicalized. After two turbulent years on campus, Dorothy dropped out and moved back to New York. She settled on the Lower East Side and took a job as a journalist for a socialist newspaper. During this period, she spent many weekends protesting against war and campaigning for women's rights. While attending one such rally outside the White House, she was arrested and went on a hunger strike with her fellow activists in prison until they were released. When her daughter was born ten years later, Dorothy began an intense period of spiritual awakening, which ultimately led her to embrace Catholicism. Her new involvement with the Catholic Church inspired her to write for Catholic publications and to work for social justice through her congregation. Her support for the peace movement remained strong and she also became actively involved in programs to feed and house the homeless. Throughout her life, Dorothy stayed fully committed to these causes—she was last arrested only five years before her death at the age of 75 for taking part in a picket line in support of striking workers.

Dolores also came to embrace activism as a way of life. She was born in New Mexico and raised in California by a single mother. Inspired by her politically active family, especially her grandfather, Dolores became engaged in a variety of causes at an early age: gathering food donations for the poor, protesting for women's rights, and organizing Mexican Independence Day celebrations and other cultural events. After earning a degree in education at a local community college, she embarked on a short-lived teaching career. Years later, Dolores reminisced that she "couldn't stand seeing kids come to class hungry and needing shoes. I thought I could do more by organizing . . . workers than by trying to teach their hungry children." Over the course of her adult life, she was married twice and had 11 children. Despite the intense demands made on her by her large family, she maintained a passionate commitment to social and political change throughout her life. To date, she has been arrested 22 times and has on many occasions been the victim of police violence.

For many, Dorothy and Dolores are the quintessential activists, showing the exceptional dedication and perseverance often associated with contentious political engagement.[1] Their biographies illustrate what some might call the nobility, and others might call the insanity, of activists. Indeed, they seem to be different from "regular people," who might care deeply about social and political issues but fail to dedicate their entire lives to a cause.

Popular accounts of activism as well as scholarly studies often focus on the actions of a few inspirational individuals like Dorothy and Dolores, who are in fact Dorothy Day (1897–1980), the founder of the Catholic Worker movement, and Dolores Huerta (born in 1930), the cofounder of the United Farm Workers with Cesar Chavez. In fact, examining the number of books written about these inspiring individuals shows that interest in charismatic leaders far outstrips attention to their movements as a whole.[2] The focus on the lives and work of this type of inspiring activist is clearly far greater than the attention given to the movements as a whole in which they engaged.

The problem with this focus on long-term, committed activists such as Dorothy and Dolores is that it misses the true story of social movement participation, substituting a charismatic leader for the movement and minimizing the significance of the vast majority of social movement participants. This clouds our larger understanding of contentious political activity and the mechanisms of social change because it implies that change results primarily from the actions of a small, homogeneous cadre instead of from a large, diverse group of individuals.

In this book I show that social movement participants are not just the dedicated few. Approximately two-thirds of the respondents from the nationally representative longitudinal study of Americans used in the analyses presented in this book have belonged to a social movement organization, attended a protest, or engaged in other forms of contentious political activity at some point in their lives. Activism, in other words, is the realm of the many. In addition, and contrary to what is sometimes assumed, social movements are not populated solely by lifelong activists. Many participants engage for only a short time and then leave altogether. Others move from group to group or reengage after a lull in participation. This is the real picture of activism, one in which many people engage, in a multitude of ways, and with varying degrees of continuity.

Karen exemplifies this type of contentious political participation. In 1974, Karen joined a student group at her high school that helped organize a march for disarmament. While working on this project, she met volunteers in the United Farm Workers, a group she would later formally join after high school in 1978. In 1982, Karen moved to Florida to help establish a National Farm Worker Ministry. However, starting in 1986, she took a long break from activism. In fact, she did not participate in social movements or contentious politics at all for 14 years. During this period, she moved to Europe, started a family, and began raising three children. Upon her return to the United States in 2000, Karen again took up the cause of social justice: she founded a Farm Worker Ministry in her church, which she still leads today.

Amy's experience is similar. In 1981, she joined a homeowners association in Santa Monica, California. This group was fighting for stricter regulation of a large homeless population in the city. Amy was on the group's board of directors and also wrote and distributed its newsletter. In 1996, she left the association after a dispute with another board member. Although there are several other similarly oriented groups in the city that she could have joined, Amy never formally returned to this cause despite her continuing concern with the large homeless population in Santa Monica. She did, however, become active in another local group that lobbies for increased funding for local schools. She continues to participate in the educational group today and also volunteers in the office of an elected state official.[3]

The biographies of Karen and Amy give a picture of activism that is very different from that portrayed by the narratives of Dorothy and Dolores. More important, Karen and Amy are much more typical activists—as the results presented in this book show, it is far more common to follow an episodic and intermittent trajectory of engagement in contentious politics than to persist over time. Like Karen and Amy, most participants move from one group to another or disengage temporarily from participation only to return later in life. Individuals follow these more intermittent trajectories as a result of both their personal characteristics and the structure and nature of the organization in which they are involved.

Thinking of activism as a process whereby people participate with varying degrees of continuity, it becomes clear that social movements and contentious political activity are part of the lives of many ordinary people. This view of social movements represents a more engaged and participatory model of democracy, one in which many individuals actively construct social change. By examining individuals who follow varying trajectories of participation, moving in and out of groups and organizations, this view also helps us to understand the rise and fall of large-scale movements over time.

Yet this type of episodic engagement is rarely the focus of studies of social movements and contentious politics. The current study reconceptualizes contentious political participation as following one of four main trajectories. Past research has identified two main trajectories of participation, which I term *persistence* and *disengagement*. Since these two trajectories are extreme opposites, they fail to capture the behavior of most participants. Therefore, I propose that there are two additional, intermediate trajectories of participation that individuals can follow: *individual abeyance*[4] and *transfer*. These two trajectories are exemplified by Karen, whose political participation was episodic, and Amy, who transferred from group to group.

An individual's trajectory of participation is the result of her ideology, resources, and biography. In addition, that trajectory is affected by the nature and structure of the social movement organization in which she is involved, which works to shape an individual's participation and the continuity of her involvement. To assess the effect of organizational structure on individual involvement, I examine three elements of organizational context: level of hierarchy, issue scope, and intensity of social interaction. Some groups are very hierarchical, while others are more egalitarian. In addition, while some groups focus on a single issue, others are based on a larger ideology that brings together a number of specific issues of concern. Finally, groups vary in the level of interaction they require; while some are based on frequent and intensive interactions, others involve only irregular and casual social contact. These three elements of organizational structure are critical for shaping the social ties and identities of participants. In turn, these ties and identities affect the length and continuity of an individual's participation.

In this book I develop and test a model that explains who will follow each of these four pathways of engagement: persistence, transfer, abeyance, and disengagement.[5] I examine this model through the use of two complementary data sources. In the first half of the book, I provide quantitative analyses of panel data originally collected by Jennings and Stoker (2004) on participation over the life course. This survey follows a nationally representative sample of high school seniors from 1965 to 1997. Through the use of these data, I examine broad predictors of initial engagement and trajectory of participation in contentious politics. In addition, I conducted 60 intensive life-history interviews with participants in four social movement organizations: a Catholic Worker group, Concerned Women for America, the United Farm Workers, and a homeowners association. These interviews allow me to examine, in greater breadth and depth than would otherwise be possible, how organizational and relational context leads individuals to follow different trajectories. These organizations and interviews are the focus of the second half of the book.

The State of Research on Participation

Scholars have consistently found that social movement participation has long-term transformative effects for individuals. Compared to nonparticipants, individuals who join social movements are likely to continue to engage in political organizations and remain consistent in their ideology over time (Downton and Wehr 1997; Giugni 2004; Klatch 1999). Previous studies, however, have largely focused on high-risk, high-cost movements and the participants who populate them, and therefore this research may not be representative of all types of engagement.[6] Given that high-risk, high-cost activism constitutes only a small fraction of all social movement organizations and activities, it is questionable whether these findings generalize to participation as a whole. In addition, while past studies have compared individuals at two points in time, once at initial engagement and once at the time of the study, they have yet to trace trajectories of participation over the life course.[7]

While research on the consequences of social movement engagement points to the potentially transformative, long-term consequences of engagement, popular opinion continues to regard social movement participation as an activity confined largely to the young. Adolescents and young adults are thought to hold more radical beliefs and to be more likely to engage in elite-challenging behavior, including joining social movements. These "radical youth" eventually develop more moderate views and leave movements as they grow older (for discussions of this popular hypothesis, see Fendrich 1993; Jennings 1987; McAdam 1988). According to this perspective, contentious participation is the result of biographical availability, and individuals are expected to move beyond this life stage as they age.

A weakness in much of the established literature is the tendency to emphasize only one phase of participation—initial engagement. This occurs despite the fact that various scholars recognize at least three stages of engagement in social movements—initial engagement, sustained participation, and disengagement (Klandermans 1997). There is, however, little research that systematically examines how and why individuals reduce their involvement in social movement organizations and protest activities.[8] Moreover, the leaving process is simply treated as identical to the joining process, only in reverse. For example, Sandell (1999, 3) states that "the decision processes concerning leaving and joining organizations are mirror images" (see also Toch 1965; Vall 1963).

This hypothesis is questionable. While there are similarities between joining and leaving a social movement organization, there are also important differences. As Veen and Klandermans (1989, 184) state, "During the period that people are associated with a movement, qualitatively new dimensions are added to being a member, so that the reasons for quitting are not the same as those for joining." Analogous situations make this point clear. For example, leaving a job is not simply the reverse of starting a job, and getting divorced is not the reverse of getting married. The emotions, relationships, and material changes associated with each transition are fundamentally different. In the same vein, increasing and decreasing one's participation in contentious politics are not mirror experiences. Hence, merely applying what we have learned about the joining process to the leaving process obscures important elements of the latter.

Rethinking Engagement: Four Trajectories of Participation

Work on the biographical consequences of participation suggests that some individuals remain active and engaged over the life course, while others leave after one episode. In this book, I present the following four prototypical trajectories that individual participants can follow after their initial engagement in contentious politics.

1. *Persistence*: Individuals remain in their initial social movement organization (SMO) and/or continue participating in protest activities over time.

2. *Transfer*: Individuals disengage from their SMO or protest activities but become active in another SMO or cause. These individuals disengage from the original movement organization but not from contentious political participation.

3. *Individual abeyance*: Individuals disengage from their SMO or protest activities but return to participation later in life.

4. *Disengagement*: Individuals permanently disengage from their SMO and from participation altogether. These individuals both leave their SMO and stop participating in collective action.

Persistence and *transfer* are similar to the processes described by McAdam (1988) in his influential study of the Freedom Summer campaign. In this campaign, mainly elite white American college students traveled from the northern states to Mississippi to register African Americans to vote during the summer of 1964. This was a transformative experience, inspiring many of the volunteers to remain politically active over the course of their lives. It is difficult, however, to assess the extent to which this experience is representative of social movement participation more generally. This campaign was extremely high in cost and risk; many volunteers experienced threats, beatings, and harassment. Three volunteers were murdered. The unusually high intensity, cost, and risk associated with this campaign suggest that it is not typical.

While the term *persistence* refers to the process of staying in the same SMO over time, the *transfer* trajectory describes moving from one social movement to another.[9] There are many reasons an individual might do this, which fall into three categories: the group may change, the individual and his interests may change, or the context may change. For example, a group may disband or begin focusing on different issues. Alternatively, an individual may move to a new city or, because of changing circumstances or maturation, may develop interests in new groups or activities. Finally, the political and social context may change, making certain issues and groups more or less salient.

The concept of social movement "spillover" is partly based on the observation that individuals often transfer their participation from group to group. Different movements and organizations within movements share personnel, and these shared personnel can move from one group to another or cooperate across groups. One result of these shifting involvements and cooperative coalitions is that a range of movement characteristics, including frames, collective identities, tactics, and elements of movement culture, can "spill over" from one group or campaign to another (Meyer and Whittier 1994).[10]

Disengagement refers to the process of permanently ceasing participation in contentious political activities. Klandermans's (1997) theoretical model of engagement in social movement organizations includes three stages of engagement: initial engagement, sustained engagement, and disengagement. These three stages, however, are intended to characterize the processes whereby individuals join and leave specific movement organizations. Through positive or negative group experiences, individuals decide to stay in or leave an organization. Many go through this process several times over the course of their lives, however, joining and leaving a range of different groups or campaigns. Here, I use the term *disengagement* to capture a permanent withdrawal from activism rather than from a particular social movement organization.

To these possibilities I add the concept of *individual abeyance*, which is intended to capture the often intermittent and fluctuating nature of contentious political participation across time. Taylor (1989) offers the concept of *movement abeyance structures* in order to highlight the continuity in SMOs and movements as a whole. In the women's movement, for example, the push for suffrage, the Equal Rights Amendment, and pay equity are often seen as distinct movements. Taylor argues, however, that these initiatives were not discrete or isolated movements; rather, they were tied together by overlapping networks of individuals, ideologies, goals, and tactics—that is, movement abeyance structures. These structures work to sustain movements under circumstances that are unfavorable to mass mobilization, as well as providing continuity from one stage of mobilization to another (Taylor 1989). Melucci et al.'s (1989) concept of submerged networks is based on a similar observation. They argue that the massive peace mobilizations of the 1980s were based on submerged networks of women, young people, ecologists, and alternative cultures. These submerged networks demonstrate that there are latent and visible poles of collective action or, more simply, moments of mass mobilization and lulls in activity.

In a similar way, episodes of participation for individuals are not discrete or isolated; they are tied together by *individual abeyance structures* over the life course.[11] Consider the participation career of Susan Brownmiller, a long-time journalist for ABC News. She initially began her activist trajectory as a volunteer for the Freedom Summer civil rights campaign. After that summer, she returned from the South and began her career in journalism; during this period, she did very little in the way of activism. Yet a number of years later she returned to social movement participation and joined the women's liberation movement (Brownmiller 1999).

I posit that these two episodes of participation by Brownmiller are not discrete and separate but instead are tied together by an individual abeyance structure that consists of networks of friends, repertoires of tactics, and ideological commitments. Brownmiller's social ties to other Freedom Summer volunteers and her leftist ideology, elements that were cultivated during her earlier participation, facilitated her subsequent reengagement. Her experience is not unique. As I argue throughout this book, many people engage episodically in this way. At a general level, examining participation over the life course can help to illuminate the ways in which individuals disengage from a particular social movement organization but not necessarily from participation as a whole, and how episodes of participation are related to one another.

A Trajectory Model of Participation

This study outlines and develops a new model of participation in social movements and contentious politics over the life course. This *trajectory model* explains participation from initial engagement through the four possible trajectories previously outlined: persistence, transfer, abeyance, and disengagement (see Figure 1 for a graphic depiction of this model).[12] The trajectory model outlines how individuals' personal characteristics lead them to initially participate in contentious politics and, once involved, how they engage within a relational and organizational context. This context shapes the identities and social ties that individuals develop in the course of engagement, which then lead them to follow different trajectories of participation.

The extensive research on initial engagement in social movements and contentious politics demonstrates that individual decisions to join organizations and participate in protest activities are the result of four sets of individual-level factors: ideology, resources, biographical availability, and social networks. Ideological factors, such as religiosity, partisanship, and efficacy, prime some individuals to participate in contentious politics. Once individuals are ideologically predisposed, however, they must have sufficient resources to allow them to translate their concern into action. Resources may be financial, such as income or wealth, or cultural, such as education or knowledge. Biographical factors can also facilitate or inhibit an individual's participation; for example, marriage, child rearing, employment, and aging may all act as barriers to participation. Finally, social networks are an important means of recruiting new members to contentious political activity. Examining all of these factors in combination enables us to understand who is most likely to engage in contentious political action. For example, are individuals who are

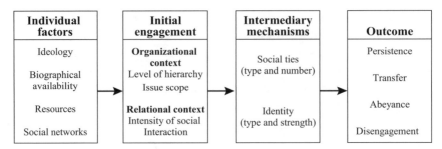

Figure 1 A trajectory model of participation

married, highly efficacious, and high income more likely than other people to participate in a social movement or protest event? How do changes in these characteristics predict an individual's shifting engagement over time?

When individuals engage in social movements or contentious politics, they do so within a specific organizational and relational context that affects their experience of participation. Clearly, not all forms of participation are equivalent. People who engage in groups where they attend a meeting once a month for an hour, who do not have friends in the organization, or who do not see the group as an important part of their overall sense of self will not experience participation in the same way as those who engage in groups where participants live communally and work for long hours each day on social movement activities.

In this study, I examine the effect of this relational and organizational context on the participation of individuals. Social movement groups vary in their relational context; some organizations require high levels of intensive social interaction among members while others require very little interaction, much of which is relatively superficial. The importance of the relational context in which individuals engage is that it influences the number and type of social ties created. In groups where members have more frequent and intensive social interaction, individuals are more likely to create strong and persistent ties. In groups where members do not interact in this way, there is a reduced chance of members bonding. A social movement that is based on strong ties, fosters those ties over the course of participation, and helps to maintain those ties after disengagement facilitates longer participation and increases the chance that an individual will reengage after a lull in engagement. Moreover, the relational context affects the types of identities that individuals create in the course of participation, as well as the salience of those identities; that is, constant and significant interaction with other group members can help to solidify relevant identities for participants.

In addition, I assess two elements of organizational context: level of hierarchy and issue scope. Groups range in their degree of hierarchy, with some being very hierarchical and others more egalitarian. In addition, while some groups focus on a single issue, others are based on a larger ideology that synthesizes a number of specific issues areas. The level of hierarchy and issue scope are critical factors affecting the development of identities among participants, and these organizational characteristics shape the identities that individuals develop in the course of participation.

I examine the variety of ways in which individuals can identify once they are involved in a social movement. They may see themselves as activists or not, as part of a particular organization or many organizations, or as proponents of different sets of values. I show that individuals who engage in the same social movement activities, such as protesting, meeting, and petitioning, may identify in very different ways, depending on their biographical characteristics and the organizational context in which their engagement takes place. The comparison of four social movement organizations in the second half of this book illustrates how the organizational and relational contexts interact with individual factors to create social ties and identities. I also examine how these ties and identities affect members' social movement and protest participation over their life course.

Data and Methods

Youth Socialization Panel Data

The Jennings and Stoker data set (2004) used in the first half of this book is an American panel study comprising a series of surveys concerning political behaviors and attitudes. A nationally representative sample of high school seniors were initially interviewed in 1965 ($N = 1669$). Subsequent surveys of the same individuals were conducted in 1973, 1982, and 1997 ($N = 934$, 56% of original sample).[13] Most important for my purposes, the survey asked individuals about their participation in both civic and community social movement organizations and activities, including demonstrating, rallying, marching, and protesting. I assess the predictors of participation by comparing individuals who have participated in a social movement group or activity with those who have not done so. These data allow me to determine the key factors that correlate with whether or not an individual has ever engaged in contentious politics, as well as to assess the predictors of shifting involvement and trajectory of participation.

Although the data are ideal for examining participation at a general level, they cannot be used to assess the role of the organizational or relational context in which participation occurs. This is because the survey did not ask about participation in specific named groups or about the structure of the group in which the respondent was involved. Yet my model of participation (Figure 1) suggests that elements of the organizational and relational context, such as issue scope, level of hierarchy, and amount of interaction in the group, play a critical role in an individual's experience of participation. Social psychological factors, such as social ties and identity, also affect an individual's decision to join[14] and, I argue, to remain in a social movement. To examine these factors, I therefore turn to intensive life-history interviews of past movement participants. The interviews demonstrate how social ties and identity act as intermediaries between organizational and relational context, on the one hand, and the trajectory of an individual's participation, on the other.

Interview Data

For the interview data used in these analyses, I recruited individuals from four social movement organizations: the United Farm Workers, a Catholic Worker group, the Concerned Women for America, and a homeowners association. Since random selection of subjects in comparative case studies can cause serious biases (Glaser and Strauss 1967; see also King et al. 1994), I selected a dimensional sample (Arnold 1970; see also Johnson 1990) of four SMOs that vary along two key dimensions: issue scope and intensity of social interaction. This approach is well suited for assessing the influence that these organizational and relational variables have on an individual's trajectory of participation.

I examine organizational scope by comparing what can be termed *multi-issue groups* with *single-issue groups*. Multi-issue groups are those that work on at least two issues that members see as connected to a larger, overarching ideology. Single-issue groups focus on one specific cause and do not explicitly tie that cause to other issues. The issue scope of a social movement organization affects the identities that participants develop and the continuity of their participation over time. I also assess the role of interaction and compare groups that have regular, intensive interactions among members with groups whose members have infrequent and less intensive interactions.

In order to examine whether these organizational factors lead individuals to take different pathways of participation, the groups represent the four possible combinations of these two variables and cover the same time period as the Jennings data. In each group, I selected 15 participants who were active in either 1970 (for the United Farm Workers and Catholic Workers) or 1980 (for the Concerned Women for America and the homeowners association).[15] I interviewed these individuals in 2005 about their participation, from their initial foray into contentious politics to the present day.[16] This research design allows me to compare individuals who remained active with those who disengaged, transferred, or had an abeyance trajectory. The demographic profile of the interview sample is similar in age and background to the quantitative panel sample and to the national population of the United States in this period.[17]

First, I examine a Catholic Worker (CW) community founded in the late 1960s and located in a large midwestern city in the United States. The Catholic Workers are involved in a variety of issues on the political left. These issues include working to resist war and imperialism abroad, as well as helping the homeless, dealing with poverty, assisting immigrants, and creating shelters for battered women in their local communities. These issues are diverse but are tied together by an overarching social justice ideology. Members engage in a high level of intensive interaction, because they live communally and tend to work six or more hours a day on volunteer activity within the group.

The second group, Concerned Women for America (CWA), is a multi-issue women's group. The participants work on a set of core issues that are connected to a more general ideology of conservative Protestant Christianity. They advocate restricting sex education in schools and promoting school prayer, protecting a traditional definition of marriage and the family and opposing gay marriage, supporting pro-life campaigns against abortion and stem-cell research, and limiting violence and sexual content in the media. There is very little interaction among members of this group, and most of the women I contacted from this organization did not know other women who were also involved in the organization. Those women who did know other members did not socialize with them or develop strong ties.

The third group, the United Farm Workers (UFW), promotes collective-bargaining rights for migrant farm workers. While many members of the UFW surely see their participation in the farm workers' struggle as part of a larger fight against inequality, the UFW is a single-issue group that works primarily on farm worker issues. Individuals in this group tend to restrict their participation to farm workers' causes, as opposed to more general leftist issues. The group of UFW members examined in this study lived communally at the union headquarters, La Paz, in California. La Paz is a physically isolated community where members interact regularly and intensively. The volunteers work on union business, up to 14 hours a day, six days a week.

The fourth group is a local community homeowners association (Homeowners Association [HA]) in Santa Monica, California,[18] established in 1981 in reaction to the perceived success of a renters' rights group in the region. The HA seeks to limit low-income housing in the area and to control what they see as a burgeoning homeless population. This single-issue group focuses mainly on protecting property values in their community through restricting the activities of the homeless.

In light of the important role of the political and social context, I also supplement the intensive interview data with historical research. Specifically, I examine newspaper accounts of the organizations, organizational publications, and biographies and autobiographies[19] of participants. Clemens and Hughes (2002) note that historical research offers distinctive advantages by allowing researchers to explore the impact of movement involvement on individual lives. The historical sources contextualize the movements politically and culturally and supplement the information provided in the interviews.

Overview of the Book

In Chapter 2, I use the panel data to examine the factors that predict whether or not a person will ever participate in a social movement organization or activity of protest, and how these factors account for shifting engagement over time. Participation in contentious politics can take a number of forms; my model assesses participation in protest activities, such as protesting, rallying, demonstrating, and marching, together with involvement in civic and community groups. Specifically, I test the role of ideology (religiosity, efficacy, and partisanship), resources (income, education, and knowledge), and biographical availability (marriage, child rearing, employment, and age), as well as a set of control variables (gender, ethnicity, and religion) in predicting engagement and shifting participation in social movements and protest over the life course.

Chapter 3 also uses the panel data, focusing more specifically on the trajectories of movement participation. I categorize all individuals who have ever participated in a social movement group or activity into one of the trajectories of participation outlined above in the trajectory model.[20] Using the trajectories as my dependent variable, I test how well the same factors that have been used to account for initial and shifting participation (from Chapter 2) explain the pattern or trajectory of participation once individuals are engaged.

The second half of the book analyzes the life-history interviews with members of the four social movement organizations. Social movement participation occurs in a relational and organizational context. This context is often impossible to examine through either large survey instruments or case studies of individual movement organizations. The importance of this context is discussed in Chapter 4 and the specific history of each of the four movement organizations is outlined in order to contextualize the respondents' participation.

In Chapter 5, I draw on the interviews to assess the role of social ties and interaction in predicting an individual's participation trajectory. The effects of ties prior to, during, and after participation in social movements are assessed as they relate to people's propensities to remain active in such groups over time. Chapter 6 focuses on the role of identity in social movement participation and the continuity of that participation over time. While past work has emphasized the development of an activist identity among individuals who participate in social movements, I show that not all individuals who engage in social movements come to define themselves as activists. In fact, individuals engaging in the same social movement activities have a variety of identity options. For example, some individuals identify with the specific movement organization in which they engage, while others more closely identify with overarching values. In this chapter, I show how organizational context and an individual's biography can lead to a variety of different identifications, and how these different identities relate to the length and continuity of participation in social movements over time.

Finally, in Chapter 7, I discuss the implications of the trajectory model of participation at the micro and macro levels. In addition, I examine how the changing nature of protest and larger cycles of protest have affected the experiences of the cohort of participants examined in this study, and how future generations of young people might experience different patterns of engagement.

2 Getting In
Initial and Shifting Engagement

PROTEST IS AN INCREASINGLY UBIQUITOUS part of life in modern industrial democracies, including the United States (Dalton 2008). From large-scale national movements to local community organizing and civic campaigns, social movements and protest participation now transcend the left-right political divide, as part of what some have called a "social movement society" (Meyer and Tarrow 1998). Indeed, the Jennings panel data show that nearly two-thirds of respondents have participated in a social movement organization or attended a protest at some point in their lives. Clearly, what were once unconventional forms of engagement are increasingly commonplace. This raises the question, why do some people come to participate in contentious politics, while others do not?

There are many reasons why individuals choose to join with others to create social change. The following four individuals illustrate the variety of those motivations. Andrew is a Latino man from a small town in California. In the late 1960s, he attended university and became friends with students involved in social justice groups; in 1969 he and his friends founded a chapter of MEChA, a Latino group focused on culture and education. While teaching Sunday school at her local church, Sally learned about Concerned Women for America and its fight against gay marriage and abortion. Believing that CWA furthered her conservative Protestant beliefs, Sally joined CWA and established a local prayer group. Sean was a pilot in the Second World War. When his plane was shot down, seriously injuring him, he came to question the use of war in foreign policy. On his return to the United States, he joined a Catholic peace group and committed himself to pacifism. Finally, Charlotte became concerned about the homeless in her community after giving birth to her first daughter in 1975. Many homeless men lived in the park near her house and she worried about her daughter's safety. Charlotte worked with other residents in her neighborhood to ban sleeping in the park and aggressive panhandling.[1]

These four people were inspired to join a social movement organization or participate in contentious politics for a variety of reasons. For Andrew, it was his social networks and his Latino identity. Religious beliefs spurred Sally's participation. Sean was fundamentally changed by his experience in war, and for Charlotte the transition to motherhood led her to join a local organization to change her community.

Although the main focus of this book is on trajectories of participation, joining a social movement group or attending an initial protest is the pivotal first step—without it, later decisions of whether to stay involved over time are irrelevant. In order to understand trajectories of participation, therefore, we must understand who initially participates. This chapter sheds light on this fundamental question by examining the roots of individual participation. Examining the predictors of initial engagement allows for a comparison of these findings with the factors that shape patterns of participation over time.

I begin with a review of the research on the key predictors of participation in contentious political activity. These include three broad types of factors: (1) ideology (religiosity, party identification, strength of partisanship, and efficacy), (2) resources (income, education, and political knowledge), and (3) biographical availability (age, marital status, child rearing, and working).

To assess how these factors influence contentious political engagement, I draw on the Jennings and Stoker panel data described in Chapter 1. The panel data set is a unique resource; it allows for a more confident test of competing theories of activism than would be possible with cross-sectional survey data. This is because we can examine variation in participation (and its predictors), both across individuals and by the same individuals over time. I do this by presenting two main panel regression models—a random effects and a fixed effects model. Through these analyses, I show that while ideological factors predispose certain individuals to become active in contentious politics, it is only those who are biographically available who are able to translate this disposition into action over time.

Predicting Social Movement Participation

The research on initial engagement in contentious politics, though broad, can be divided into three main approaches that focus on ideological factors, resources, and biographical availability, respectively (see Figure 1).[2] Ideological factors are critical for creating sympathy toward a movement's goals—a necessary but insufficient condition for movement participation. Once there is sympathy for a group or cause, only those with the necessary resources and who are biographically available will be able to convert their sympathy into action. After describing the predictors of initial engagement, I examine how changes in these factors will predict shifting involvement in and out of contentious politics over time.

Ideological Factors

Recent work on contentious political participation has recognized that engagement is a two-step process. The first step is a generalized sympathy with or commitment to the goals and tactics of a movement (Klandermans and Oegema 1987; Oegema and Klandermans 1994). While it may seem obvious that sympathy with a movement's goals and methods is necessary for activism, sympathy alone is not sufficient to spur one to action. At the same time, it is important to understand how ideological factors "prime" one to participate. I examine several ideological factors including partisanship, religiosity, and feelings of efficacy. Individuals who have strong partisan attachments, are religious, and feel politically efficacious can be seen as having stronger beliefs. Social movements and contentious politics are one outlet for these ideologies and beliefs, allowing individuals to voice their concerns.

First, social movements have long been associated with the Left. Movements such as those for women's rights, for civil rights, on behalf of labor, against war, and to protect the environment have led to significant social change. Because of these widespread mobilizations, protest is often seen as an important means by which leftists can challenge those who hold power. Research in the United States and elsewhere supports this argument, showing that liberals are more likely than other people to report participating in protest (Dalton 2008; Dalton et al. 2010; Hirsch 1990). Alternatively, recent events in the United States, including the rise of the religious Right, suggest that committed individuals on either the left or right are more likely than others to engage in political activity, including protest. Lee (1997) finds that ideological orientations are important factors that predispose individuals toward political extremism and are significant predictors of activism (see also Muller and Jukam 1977). My analysis will test the role of political ideology, in terms of both left-right orientation and ideological polarization.

Second, religiosity predicts a wide range of behaviors, including engagement in contentious political activity. Religious institutions have been important in many social movement campaigns throughout American history: Quakers played a central role in the abolition of slavery, evangelical churches were active in temperance and moral reform campaigns, mainline Protestant churches were cornerstones of the 1960s antiwar movement, and African American Protestant churches fostered the growth of the civil rights movement (Greenberg 2000).

The reason why religiosity fosters activism is that belonging to and participating in a religious institution is associated with an orientation toward the collective good. In addition, connection to a community of like-minded believers provides the moral impetus to engage in collective action for social change. As a result, individuals who are strongly connected to their communities through religious institutions are more likely to join social movements (Diani 2004; Gould 1990; McAdam 1986). It should be noted, however, that some work has found that religious values are associated with conservative beliefs (Luker 1984; Page and Clelland 1978), and many religious institutions focus on conformity and obedience, which can suppress participation (Ellison and Sherkat 1993).

Religious affiliation is also related to one's propensity to engage in social movements. For example, Snow and Oliver (1993) find that people who are Catholic or Jewish, because of their historical experiences as minority groups in the United Sates, are more likely to have participated in the protests of the 1960s; other research on activism in later time periods supports this finding (Sherkat and Blocker 1993). It is also clear that social gospel and liberation theology in Catholicism can serve as an ideological frame that legitimizes progressive social justice work (Smith 1991). In contrast, evangelical Protestants are particularly unlikely to engage in protest activity (Beyerlein and Hipp 2006). Beyond the role of religiosity, which measures the strength or behavioral expression of religious preference, religious affiliation can also shape activism over the life course.

Political efficacy is also important for movement participation. Efficacy is the belief that one is capable of the specific behaviors required to produce a desired outcome in a given situation (Gecas 2000). A high level of efficacy indicates that individuals feel self-confident, believe they are causal agents in their environment, and consequently are able to produce the changes in the world that they desire. Research suggests that there is a positive relationship between efficacy and participation in protest activity (Klandermans et al. 2008; Rosenstone and Hansen 1993; Teixeira 1992).[3]

Resources

While the ideologies discussed above, such as being religious, leftist, or efficacious, increase the propensity to participate in contentious political activity, ideology alone is not enough. Individuals must also have the necessary resources to translate these beliefs into action and must be willing to bear the costs associated with fighting for a cause. As a result, individuals who have certain kinds of resources, such as money, education, and/or knowledge, are more likely to participate in collective action.

Socioeconomic status is a critical predictor of participation in both contentious politics and traditional political activity. Proponents of resource mobilization theory argue that grievances alone are not enough to lead to collective action. Instead, in order to mobilize, individuals and groups require access to and control over resources (McCarthy and Zald 1977). Verba et al. (1995) also emphasize the importance of resources in their Civic Voluntarism Model. This model focuses on the role of socioeconomic status (SES) and shows that high SES provides the critical resources, such as time, money, and civic skills, which enable individuals to participate in politics and social movements.[4] Because of this, individuals with higher SES are more likely to engage in political activity and in civic groups of all kinds, including social movement organizations (see also Leighley and Nagler 1992; Putnam 2000; Rosenstone and Hansen 1993).

In addition to monetary resources, education has a positive relationship with protest (Crozat 1998; Dalton 2008). Similarly, political knowledge increases protest activity. Putnam's work on political participation and general group membership shows that political knowledge is a "critical precondition for active forms of participation," and those who know more about politics are more likely to engage in protest (Putnam 2000, 35). The importance of SES, political knowledge, and education for predicting engagement can be taken as evidence that protest is at least partially a function of personal resources.

Biographical Availability

The concept of biographical availability has long been central to studies of differential recruitment. It is only when individuals are biographically available to participate in contentious politics that they will be able to convert their beliefs and resources into political action (Beyerlein and Hipp 2006). Individuals experience life-cycle changes that make them more or less available to participate. For example, some personal constraints, such as family responsibilities or full-time employment, might increase the costs and risks of movement participation (McAdam 1986, 70). In addition, when individuals are performing certain kinds of roles, such as the role of parent or spouse, the commitments associated with these roles might limit their availability to participate in social movements (Rochford 1985; Snow et al. 1986). Therefore, individuals with fewer responsibilities and constraints are more likely to have the time, energy, and inclination to engage in contentious political activity.[5]

There are several specific role and life-cycle changes that affect an individual's decision or ability to engage in collective action. Marriage, for example, implies a commitment to one's spouse that may supersede loyalties to a movement. In addition, marriage often coincides with other major life events, such as geographical moves, job changes, and having children, that may reduce the time available for activism (Stoker and Jennings 1995). Finally, the array of new responsibilities and dependencies that generally accompany marriage may also reduce the willingness of many married people to engage in risky forms of participation that could result in arrest or other punishments. Wiltfang and McAdam's (1991) research supports these hypotheses and finds that those who have never been married tend to give more time to activism than those who have been married.

Becoming a parent is also a significant life-cycle change that could affect an individual's political participation. When examined from the biographical availability perspective, we would expect that individuals with children would be less likely to participate in contentious politics (Oliver 1984). Family responsibilities can decrease the free time available for collective action as well as the willingness to take the risks associated with activism. Empirical findings, however, are mixed. Some studies find that having children is a positive predictor of social movement participation (Wiltfang and McAdam 1991; Wright and Hyman 1958) but others have found it to be a negative or neutral predictor (Ahlbrandt and Cunningham 1979; Corrigall-Brown et al. 2009; Oliver 1984).

These contradictory results suggest that the context of a movement organization may shape patterns of social activism. Movement organizations require varying amounts of time and energy; those that require more from members may discourage parents from participating. Similarly, movement organizations involve different levels of risk. Most SMOs in North America today are low risk and low cost and would therefore not be incompatible with child rearing. This was probably less true in past campaigns, such as the civil rights, antiwar, and women's movements, which have been the focus of many past studies. However, protest and social movement activity have evolved significantly in recent decades as they have become an increasingly conventional form of participation. Protest events and marches are often coordinated with local police and even arrests of activists are often planned in advance (McPhail et al. 1998).[6]

In addition to the overall routinization of protest, engagement in a movement cause that is supportive of the values and needs of the family can make getting married and having children compatible with activism. This can be the case, for example, in some movement organizations on the religious Right that are based on support for "traditional family values." For example, many women who participated in Concerned Women for America, a conservative religious women's group that is one of the four groups examined in the latter half of this book, saw their membership in the group as a part of supporting the traditional nuclear family. For these women, marrying and having children increased their commitment to the values of the group and therefore helped to encourage participation (for a similar finding, see Luker's [1984] work on the prochoice and pro-life movements). Much work on the concept of maternal activism argues that the intersection of motherhood and political activism has a long history in a multiplicity of movements (see, e.g., Connolly 2004; McDonald 1997; Peteet 1997).

In addition to changes in family circumstances, individuals also experience transitions in employment status over the course of their lives that may affect their ability to engage in activism. McCarthy and Zald (1973), for example, hypothesize that those free of employment pressures, such as students, retirees, and the unemployed, are more likely to participate in contentious politics. Those with more flexible jobs are also thought to be more likely to engage. Interestingly, however, empirical research has largely contradicted these expectations. McAdam (1986) and Nepstad and Smith (1999) find that those who are employed full-time and in less flexible jobs are actually more likely to engage in protest. This is partly explained by resources associated with employment, which predict participation and may offset the effect of a restricted schedule.[7]

Finally, age is an important source of biographical availability that may play an independent role in shaping engagement. On the one hand, younger people tend to be free of family and employment constraints that could hinder political activity (Wiltfang and McAdam 1991). On the other hand, older people are less likely to have children at home and more likely to be retired (Nepstad and Smith 1999). In this way, both younger and older people tend to have more free time and fewer constraints on their activism. Past work on social movement participation demonstrates this curvilinear relationship between age and engagement (Beyerlein and Hipp 2006).

In summary, biographical availability theory leads us to expect that individuals with more free time should be more likely to engage in social movements and protest. However, much of the empirical research in this area has found just the opposite—individuals who are married, parents, and employed are more likely to participate in these groups and activities. In this analysis, I examine how biographical availability enables individuals to engage in contentious politics and how shifts in this availability over time alter one's propensity to engage over the life course.

Sociodemographic Factors

Sociodemographic characteristics such as gender and race are often used as control variables in analyses of differential recruitment. The role of gender in movement engagement has been extensively examined and, in general, prior work shows that women are less likely than men to participate in social movements (Cable 1992; Lee 1997; McAdam 1992; Rochford 1985). There are several possible reasons why women are less involved. Women are commonly asked to perform menial, personally unrewarding tasks in social movements (Cable 1992; McAdam 1992; Thorne 1975). This may reduce the attraction of participation. Women's relative participation increases, however, in movement organizations where their contributions are more valued, such as feminist organizations or community groups.

The role of race and ethnicity in political activism has also been widely studied, but this research has yielded mixed findings. It is clear that ethnicity and SES overlap, with African Americans having, on average, lower socioeconomic status than whites in the United States. And, as SES is strongly correlated with social movement participation, we would expect this would suppress the participation of African Americans. When controlling for SES, however, most studies find that African Americans have higher rates of participation than whites (Babchuk and Thompson 1962; McPherson 1977; Olsen

1970). It is important to note that these studies were conducted following the height of the civil rights movement in the United States, a time of considerable political activity in the African American community. More recent studies find that African Americans are less likely to engage in protest behavior (Sherkat and Blocker 1993).[8]

Data and Methods

The Jennings and Stoker data are a nationally representative longitudinal probability sample of high school seniors first interviewed in 1965 ($N = 1669$). Subsequent surveys of the same individuals were conducted in 1973, 1982, and 1997 ($N = 934$, 56% of original sample). Detailed information about the sampling procedure and loss of respondents over time may be found in the Appendix.

Dependent Variable

Respondents were asked a variety of political participation questions, including whether they had participated in a protest, demonstration, rally, or march, and if they had been a member of a politically oriented civic or community group in each of the four time periods. More specifically, as defined by Jennings and Stoker in their survey instrument, civic groups are "non-partisan or civic groups interested in the political life of the community" and community groups are "groups that work to solve a community problem."[9] The dependent variable is simply whether or not an individual had participated in one of these activities or was a member of a civic or community group in each of the four survey periods.[10]

Independent Variables and Scale Construction

Resources   I include three measures of resources: family income, education, and political knowledge. Family income is converted into 1997 dollars, the last year of the survey, for comparability across time. This variable was logged in each of the four periods. Education is operationalized as years of postsecondary education, as all individuals in this study had attained grade 12 because the initial 1965 sample included only high school seniors. The education variable ranges from 0 to 7, with 7 indicating seven or more years of postsecondary education. Political knowledge is assessed by counting the number of correct answers to a series of six questions about politics.[11] The scale ranges from low knowledge (0 correct) to high knowledge (6 correct).

Ideology   Ideological factors were assessed with five measures: party identification, strength of partisanship, religiosity, religious denomination, and efficacy. Party identification runs from 0 (strong Democrat) to 6 (strong Republican).[12] I use the same question to create a "strength of partisanship" variable. Folding the party identification scale, the result is a measure ranging from 0 to 3, with 0 indicating moderate and 3 indicating the furthest on each extreme. Religiosity is operationalized as the frequency of church attendance, ranging from 0 (not religious) to 5 (religious and attend weekly).[13] Religious denomination is controlled for with Protestants as the reference category.

The political efficacy measure is created from two questions. The respondents were asked if they either agree or disagree with the following two statements: "I don't think public officials care much what people like me think" and "People like me don't have any say about what the government does."[14] Efficacy ranges from 0 (low) to 4 (high).

Biographical availability   There are four measures of biographical availability: age, marriage, child rearing, and employment. Age is derived from a question on year of birth. I also include an age-squared term to test for a curvilinear relationship between age and contentious activity. Three biographical changes are assessed: marriage, child rearing, and employment. I code marital status into three categories: single; married or living with an opposite sex partner;[15] and separated, divorced, or widowed. For child rearing, a variable counting the number of children in the home is created. This measure ranges from 0 to 6, with the latter category including those with six or more children in the home.[16] Employment is measured as the number of hours per week respondents are employed. This variable ranges from 0 hours per week, if they are unemployed, to 90 hours, indicating 90 hours or more per week. As for age, I also include a squared term to test for a curvilinear effect.

Methods

To test the competing theories discussed above, I present two models below. To limit missing data and prevent bias in the findings, I used the Amelia program designed by Honaker et al. (version 1.2-15) to create multiple imputations of the missing data.[17] I created five imputed data sets and ran logistic panel data analyses with each of the imputed data sets. This model type takes into account the dichotomous dependent variable and controls for the fact that with longitudinal data each observation is not independent; instead, the same individual is observed at four separate points in time. I ran the models on each of the five imputed data sets and averaged the results for the final findings.

I present two types of logistic panel data models—a random effects model and a fixed effects model—in order to get a more complete picture of engagement over time. The random effects model provides a general picture of the factors associated with contentious political activity and looks at both cross-sectional and over-time variance. In essence, this model shows why some people participate while others do not (cross-sectional variation) and why individuals move in and out of engagement (over-time variation). This model helps us to understand who will ever engage in a social movement group or activity.

The fixed effects model, in contrast, only examines the factors that explain over-time variance in participation or, in other words, why the same individual may participate at one point in time but not at another (for a discussion of these statistical models, see Wooldridge 2001). The fixed effects model does not examine variables that do not change, such as gender or race. In effect, this model helps assess the predictors of who will move in and out of social movement participation over the course of their lives. This model allows me to test one of my main research questions: How do changing ideologies, resources, and biographical availability affect an individual's participation over time? By comparing the results of the random effects model (which examines over-time and cross-sectional variance) and the fixed effects model (which only examines over-time variance), I can isolate the factors that predict who will ever engage from those that predict changing participation over time.

An Examination of Participation

Sixty-five percent of the individuals in this sample have participated in either a social movement organization or a protest activity during at least one period over the four waves of the survey (see Figure 2). Despite stereotypes of social movement participants as being a fringe group, this finding demonstrates that participation in contentious political activity is not simply the purview of a small group of individuals. In fact, a majority of Americans will engage in these activities or groups at some point in their lives. Evidently, contentious political activity is part of the political repertoire of a large number of individuals.

As Figure 2 shows, individuals who have engaged in contentious politics are most likely to have participated during only one time period (30%) (ei-

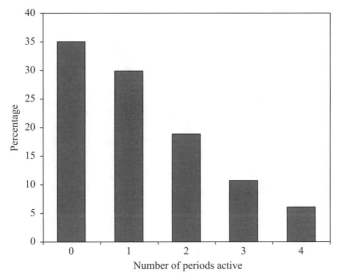

Figure 2 Percentage of respondents by number of survey periods active in contentious politics

ther before 1965, from 1966 to 1973, from 1974 to 1982, or from 1983 to 1997). While 19 percent participated during two time periods, only 11 percent and 6 percent participated during three or four time periods, respectively. Therefore, while 65 percent of the individuals in this sample have participated in a social movement group or protest activity at least once over the four waves of the panel data collection, most people do not engage in each and every period throughout their lives. This indicates that individuals are moving in and out of contentious political activity over the life course instead of remaining active from period to period.

Figure 3 demonstrates that there was a rise in engagement from 1965 (when the respondents were 18 years old) to 1982 (when the respondents were 35) and then a decline in the final time period (1997, when respondents were 50). This pattern of participation is consistent with larger cycles of protest in the United States over this time frame, which saw a high level of protest from the 1960s to the end of the 1970s. This peak period was followed by a lull in protest activities at the national level (Larson and Soule 2009). The larger cycles of protest are mirrored in the individual experiences of my sample.[18] The ways in which the individual patterns of participation reflect macrocycles of protest illustrate how a better understanding of individual engagement can illuminate social movement processes on a larger scale.

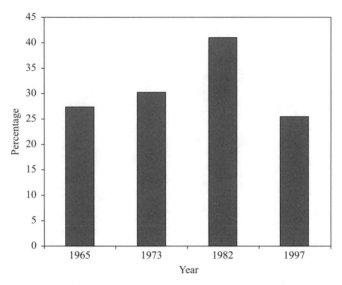

Figure 3 Percentage of respondents active in contentious politics by survey year

Who is this sizeable group that participates in contentious politics? Table 1 shows that individuals who have participated differ from those who have not in a number of respects. In general, participants are more likely to be female (by 11%), black (by 5%), and Jewish (by 3%) than are nonparticipants. Participants differ from those who do not engage in terms of their ideology: they are more religious and attend church more often than nonparticipants (3.001 compared with 2.674 on a five-point scale). They are also, on average, more efficacious than nonparticipants, scoring a mean of 2.113 on the four-point scale compared with 1.829 for nonparticipants. Participants are also slightly more likely to be Democrats and to be strongly partisan. Comparison of the participants with nonparticipants also shows that those who engage have more resources than those who do not. They have, on average, incomes that are over $15,000 more in each period than nonparticipants; they have approximately an additional half year of postsecondary education; and they answer about 0.5 additional questions correctly on the political knowledge test. Biographically, the overwhelming majority of both participants and nonparticipants marry and have children. However, consistent with the wide range of work on the biographical consequences of activism, participants are less likely to marry (by 4%) and less likely to have children (by 12%) than those who have never engaged.

Table 1 Comparison of total sample and participants in contentious political action

		Nonparticipants		Participants only*	
		Mean	Percent	Mean	Percent
Ideology					
Religiosity	(0 = Not Rel., 5 = Weekly+)	2.674 (1.048)		3.001 (1.083)	
Party identification	(0 = Str. Dem., 6 = Str. Rep.)	2.897 (0.987)		2.766 (1.484)	
Strength of partisanship	(0 = Weak, 3 = Strong)	0.988 (1.829)		1.062 (0.995)	
Efficacy	(0 = Low, 4 = High)	1.829 (0.422)		2.113 (0.538)	
Resources					
Income	1997 dollars	32492.56 (20524.95)		47970.65 (22321.97)	
Postsecondary education	(0 = 0 years, 7 = 7+ years)	0.938 (1.683)		1.398 (2.013)	
Political knowledge	(0 = Low, 6 = High)	3.845 (2.674)		4.362 (1.170)	
Biographical availability					
Marital status	Never married		6.3		10.4
	Has been married		93.8		89.6
Children	Never had children		16.8		28.4
	Had children		83.2		71.6
Work hours	(0 = 0 hours, 90 = 90+ hours)	21.339 (13.298)		20.594 (12.317)	
Control variables					
Gender	Female		41.9		52.3
	Male		58.1		47.7
Race	White		96.6		91.2
	Black		2.4		7.6
	Other		1.0		1.2
Religion	Protestant		67.0		68.5
	Catholic		24.6		20.7
	Jewish		2.0		5.3
	Other		0.8		1.0
	None		5.6		4.5

NOTE: Numbers in parentheses are standard deviations.

*Individuals who participated in an act of protest or social movement organization in one or more periods.

Multivariate Findings

Predicting Ever Engaging

The logistic panel model with random effects is presented in Table 2. This model shows, at a general level, the impact of the independent variables on whether or not an individual has ever engaged in contentious politics. It includes all the respondents at each of the four points in time, including those who moved in and out of contentious politics and those who either never participated or were active in each period over the life course. There are three main groups of findings in this model.

First, when controlling for other factors, religious individuals are less likely to have engaged in contentious politics. One additional point on the religiosity scale (0–5) decreases an individual's chance of participating by a factor of 0.920. This is notable given the importance of religion in past social movement campaigns. Movements, such as those for civil rights, against war, and for other social justice issues, have often been fostered within churches (Greenberg 2000). It seems, however, that being religious is not sufficient to lead to participation, despite the fact that religiosity may foster social ties and resources that are associated with engagement. Instead, religion can act as an alternative outlet of action for some. For example, many members of Concerned Women for America who were interviewed for the second half of this book were highly religious but chose to express their concern about social issues through their churches instead of traditional social movements. Religious organizations may, in this way, sometimes encourage individuals to focus on changing themselves or their immediate social circle instead of trying to alter the larger society through contentious political action.

Political party identification also affects the likelihood of participation. Each additional point to the right on the political party identification scale (0–6) decreases the likelihood of participating by a factor of 0.791. This finding is consistent with past work, which finds that liberals are more likely to engage in social movement groups and tactics, such as protest (see, e.g., Dalton 2008; Dalton et al. 2010). With the rise of conservative movements in the United States, such as the Tea Party movement, and the way in which these groups increasingly have come to embrace traditional social movement tactics, this relationship might change over time for later cohorts. It should also be noted that the intensity of ideology is not related to engagement—it is only whether one is left or right, not how strongly one identifies either way, that predicts participation.

Table 2 Random and fixed effects models predicting engagement in contentious politics

	Random effects model			Fixed effects model		
	Coefficient	Standard error	Odds	Coefficient	Standard error	Odds
Constant	1.485	(1.417)				
Ideology						
Religiosity	−0.083*	(0.037)	0.920	0.003	(0.062)	1.003
Party identification	−0.234***	(0.033)	0.791	−0.230	(0.052)	0.795
Strength of partisanship	0.084	(0.058)	1.088	0.044	(0.087)	1.045
Efficacy	0.166*	(0.078)	1.181	0.004	(0.113)	1.004
Resources						
Income (logged)	0.100	(0.083)	1.105	0.013	(0.111)	1.013
Education	0.080**	(0.027)	1.083	0.024	(0.035)	1.024
Political knowledge	0.162***	(0.046)	1.176	0.065	(0.079)	1.067
Biographical availability						
Age	−0.272***	(0.064)	0.762	−0.173*	(0.077)	0.841
Age squared	0.003***	(0.001)	1.003	0.003*	(0.001)	1.003
Single	0.349 *	(0.165)	1.418	1.067***	(0.260)	2.907
Married (omitted category)						
Separated/ divorced/ widowed	0.281*	(0.178)	1.324	0.506*	(0.240)	1.659
Children	0.119*	(0.054)	1.126	0.123*	(0.060)	1.131
Work hours	0.048***	(0.007)	1.049	0.038***	(0.009)	1.039
Work hours squared	−0.001***	(0.001)	0.999	−0.002***	(0.001)	0.998
Control variables						
Gender	0.682***	(0.132)	1.978			
White (omitted category)						
Black	1.232***	(0.228)	3.428			
Other minority	0.906*	(0.461)	2.474			
Protestant (omitted category)						
Catholic	0.204	(0.145)	1.226	−0.511	0.361	0.600
Jewish & other religions	0.479	(0.285)	1.614	0.975	0.914	2.651

*$p < 0.05$
**$p < 0.01$
***$p < 0.001$

The last ideological factor in this model, efficacy, is a positive predictor of engagement; those who score one point higher on the efficacy scale (ranging from 0 to 4) are 1.181 times more likely to participate in contentious political activity. It is not surprising that individuals who feel that their actions are more likely to produce change will have a higher propensity to engage in groups and activities aimed at making these changes. The significance of this factor emphasizes the importance of individuals' beliefs about their ability to shape their social world.

Second, cultural resources are important predictors of engagement in this model. While the nonmonetary resources of education and political knowledge are significant predictors of engagement, income is not associated with one's propensity to participate in contentious action. Education is a positive predictor of engagement; individuals who have a four-year postsecondary degree are 1.38 times more likely to have engaged in contentious politics than those who have only a high school diploma. Knowledge is also a significant predictor of participation: those who answered four questions correctly on the political knowledge test are over 1.38 times more likely to have engaged than those who answered only two questions correctly. Education and knowledge are important because they allow individuals to learn about social issues, campaigns, and events. The effects of education and knowledge are distinct, as controlling for one does not mitigate the effect of the other. So, education is important not only because it increases knowledge but also because of other benefits it brings, which could include facilitating movement into professions that are more likely to be associated with civic involvement and/or facilitating access to divergent opinions and information.

Financial resources, however, are not significantly related to one's likelihood of engaging in contentious politics. This is surprising given the importance of financial resources in past work for predicting both traditional political participation and contentious political activity (see, e.g., Leighley and Nagler 1992; Rosenstone and Hansen 1993; Verba et al. 1995). Nonetheless, when controlling for factors that are associated with income, such as gender, race, education, and knowledge, income is not a significant predictor of participation.

Finally, the most significant predictors of whether an individual has ever engaged in a social movement are biographical. Age, marriage, child rearing, and working are all significant predictors of who will engage in contentious politics in this model. Marriage decreases one's chance of participating

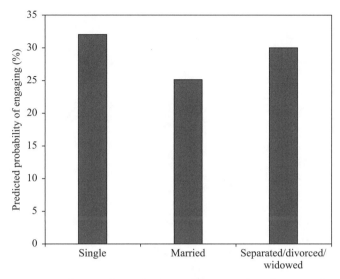

Figure 4 Percentage chance of engaging in contentious politics by marital status*
*Estimated probabilities for a white, Protestant female working full-time with all other variables held at their mean.

in this analysis. Individuals who are single and those who are separated, widowed, or divorced are 1.324 times more likely to have engaged than those who are married.

In Figure 4, I illustrate this relationship by comparing a white, Protestant, single female with one who is married and one who is separated, divorced, or widowed. Holding all other characteristics at their mean values, she has a 32 percent chance of participating if she is single, a 25 percent chance of participating if she is married, and a 30 percent chance of participating if she is separated, divorced, or widowed. In this way, those who remain single and those who were married but are no longer are most likely to engage. It is the *state* of being married that suppresses participation.

Contrary to expectations based on past work, however, the number of children in the home is a *positive* predictor of engagement. Each additional child increases one's chance of participating by a factor of 1.226. This could be because being a parent encourages certain types of activism, such as engagement in groups concerned with education or other issues related to children.

Work hours are positively associated with engagement in social movements and contentious politics. However, the relationship between work hours and engagement is curvilinear. Individuals at the top and the bottom—

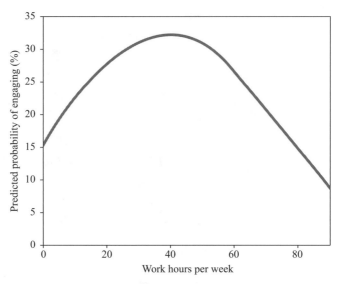

Figure 5 Percentage chance of engaging in contentious politics by work hours per week. Estimated probabilities for a white, Protestant female with all other variables held at their mean.

those either working a lot or not at all—are the least likely to engage. As illustrated in Figure 5, those who work full-time (40 hours per week) are the most likely to engage. A white, Protestant woman with all other variables held at their mean who works 40 hours a week has a 32 percent chance of participating. If this same white, Protestant female does not work at all for pay, she has only a 16 percent chance of participating. And if she works 70 hours a week, her chance of engaging rises to 21 percent. The curvilinear relationship illuminates some of the contradictory findings of past work. On the one hand, those with no work constraints, such as students and stay-at-home parents, do not have the social ties and resources associated with work that could facilitate engagement. On the other hand, those who work more than full-time cannot engage because of their restricted schedules. Thus the most likely participants are those who are employed but do not work excessively.

The relationship between age and protest engagement is also curvilinear, with individuals in the middle-age category less likely to engage. This finding is consistent with the findings for work hours and marital status. The study's participants were students in the late 1960s, when it was much less common for students to work for pay while attending school (Bradley 2006). Young people were more likely to be free of paid employment and be single, both of which are predictors of engagement. In the same way, the later age groups are more likely to be retired or separated/divorced/widowed, all of which are associated with a higher propensity to engage in contentious political action.

This analysis also shows that women were almost twice as likely as men to have participated in contentious political activity. In addition, whites are less likely to have engaged than African Americans and those of other races, who were 3.428 times and 2.474 times more likely to participate, respectively. These relationships exist when controlling for education, knowledge, and income, all of which are highly correlated with race in the United States.

Predicting Shifting Engagement

The fixed effects model allows for a more specific assessment of the causes of changes in participation over time and for consideration of how the independent variables—ideology, resources, and biography—are associated with these changes. This model examines the factors that predict moving in and out of contentious political activity. Through examining individuals whose participation has changed over time, we can see how changes in the independent variables affect engagement in contentious politics.

This model highlights the importance of biographical changes in predicting shifting engagement over the life course. The random effects model shows that ideology is an important predictor of who will engage in contentious politics; individuals who are leftist, less religious, and more efficacious are more likely to participate in contentious politics at some point in their lives. The random effects model also highlights the importance of nonmonetary resources, such as education and knowledge, for predicting engagement. In the fixed effects model, however, we find that ideology and resources are not significant predictors and appear to play little role in individuals' moving in and out of contentious politics over time.

The statistical insignificance of these variables in the fixed effects model illustrates how ideological factors and resources are best viewed as primers for political participation; while only individuals who are ideologically predisposed and have resources will engage, ideological commitment and resources alone are not sufficient to cause engagement. Instead, biographical availability is needed to translate ideology and resources into action.

Changes in biographical availability are related to movement in and out of contentious political activity. Consider, for example, the findings on marital status. In their analysis, Wiltfang and McAdam (1991) found that individuals who are married are less likely to engage in protest. I also find a negative relationship between marriage and engagement but show that it is, in fact, the transition to marriage that suppresses participation. Individuals who are single are 2.907 times more likely to engage than those who have married.

But what happens when previously married people later separate, divorce, or become widowed? In short, they behave much more like they did when they were single. In fact, individuals who were once married but are not anymore are over 1.659 times more likely to engage in contentious political activity than those who are still married. In other words, while marriage suppresses participation, the results indicate that the state of being married is the critical factor. Changes in one's marital status, from single to married or married to single, shift one's propensity to engage in contentious politics. Past work has only been able to examine the effect of the *state* of being married on participation. The findings presented in Table 2 address how *changes* in marital status shape one's participation over time.

As in the random effects model, the fixed effects model demonstrates the positive relationship between child rearing and participation. When controlling for marital status, having children increases the likelihood of participating in contentious politics, and the addition of each child to the household increases one's likelihood of participating by a factor of 1.131. Thus, it is not simply that individuals who are active in contentious politics are more likely to have children at some point in their lives, but that having children leads to increased participation. While past work on the biographical consequences of activism and follow-up studies of activists has demonstrated the effects of engagement on marrying and child rearing—often finding that it suppresses both—this analysis adds to the literature by showing that not only does activism affect biography but also that biography affects activism.

Individuals who work more are more likely to participate in contentious politics by a factor of 1.039. As in the random effects model, however, this relationship is curvilinear; those who do not work at all or those who are employed and work more than full-time are the least likely to have engaged in contentious politics. The impact of age on participation is also curvilinear. Those who are very young and those who are in the oldest age category are most likely to engage in protest. As individuals age they tend to leave contentious politics and then later return. This finding shows the importance of focusing on intermittent, or abeyance, patterns of participation over time, showing how the process of aging is related to moving in and out of political activity. Only through examining initial predictors of participation and showing how changes in these predictors shape participation over time is it possible to assess the role of the biographical changes examined in this analysis.

Discussion and Conclusion

Contentious political activity is part of the lives of a majority of Americans. In fact, 65 percent of the nationally representative sample in this study has either participated in a social movement organization or activity of protest. Engagement in contentious politics is clearly widespread; protest is part of the social and political repertoire of the majority of citizens. The aim of this chapter is to examine who engages in collective action and assess how changes in ideology, resources, and biographical availability over the life course affect one's propensity to move in and out of activism. There are three main findings.

First, while ideological factors are important predictors of initial engagement in protest, they are not strongly associated with the propensity to move in and out of contentious political activity. Clearly, ideology primes participation in contentious politics. This finding is consistent with past work that highlights the importance of sympathy toward a movement as a critical precursor to activism (Beyerlein and Hipp 2006; Oegema and Klandermans 1994). While individuals will not participate without a sympathetic ideological orientation, however, these orientations alone are insufficient to cause participation. Instead, resources and biographical availability are required for individuals to engage in contentious political action and sustain that action over time.

Second, this analysis illuminates the role of different types of resources in predicting participation over the life course. Those who have more education and knowledge are more likely to engage. However, financial resources, which past work has repeatedly found to be critical predictors of political participation (Leighley and Nagler 1992; Rosenstone and Hansen 1993; Verba et al. 1995), are not significant predictors of engagement or shifting involvement.

Third, biographical factors are strongly related to one's propensity to participate. The curvilinear relationship of work hours and age to participation and the impact of marital changes on participation demonstrate how shifts in biographical availability influence an individual's ability to translate ideological sympathy into contentious political action. The importance of biographical factors underscores the main argument of this book: only by examining individuals over the life course can we understand individual participation and the rise and fall of movements over time.

This book offers a typology of trajectories of participation in social movements and contentious politics. In order to understand a person's trajectory of participation over time, we must begin by assessing who engages initially and why she chooses to do so. This chapter sheds light on this fundamental question by examining the roots of individual participation in social movement organizations and protest activities. Once individuals have made the decision to join or participate, they are faced later with decisions of whether or not to stay involved. To what extent do the factors that lead to their initial engagement influence their decision whether to stay involved over time? This examination of shifting involvement pushes us beyond looking only at predictors of initial engagement. The next chapter builds on these analyses by examining the patterns or trajectories that participation may follow. Though there has been some research in this area, it has been limited to explanations at the individual level and to one social movement organization at a time. I build on this literature by assessing trajectories of participation in a variety of social movement organizations and activities over an individual's life course.

3 Trajectories of Participation

ALTHOUGH A MAJORITY OF AMERICANS HAVE PARTICIPATED in social movements or contentious politics at some point in their lives, only some have been fundamentally transformed by their participation and become committed, lifelong activists. Certainly this was the case for Sylvia and James, a young married couple who went to La Paz, the United Farm Workers' headquarters, in 1966, to donate food to the striking workers. Sylvia and James had always been concerned with social justice and had volunteered for charitable organizations, including an orphanage and a food bank. At La Paz, they heard a speech given by Cesar Chavez and were inspired by a group of Filipino farm workers they met. Sylvia recounts how she and James sat silently on the drive home, transfixed by their experience. They sold all their possessions and moved to La Paz in order to work full-time for the union. As Sylvia recounted, this meeting "changed the course of my life."

Sylvia and James lived at La Paz for 12 years until Sylvia became ill. She was diagnosed with cancer and, in order to be closer to medical care, Sylvia, James, and their two children moved to San Diego to live with her extended family. While Sylvia received treatment for her illness, both she and James remained active volunteers in a group that worked to include Cesar Chavez and the history of the farm worker movement in the California school curriculum. After Sylvia recovered from her illness, she and James started running an organization that lobbies the government for increased funding for education and a more multicultural curriculum.

For both Sylvia and James, their first trip to La Paz was transformational and led them to radically alter the course of their lives. Their biographies mirror the narratives of many activists, including those of Dorothy Day and Dolores Huerta, discussed in the Introduction. However, not all who participate in a social movement organization or attend a protest event are transformed by the experience and become lifelong activists. Indeed, that is the exception. With this in mind, this chapter examines the ways in which individuals participate in contentious politics over time and the different trajectories participation can take over the life course.

Examining the full range of participatory trajectories, including more intermittent and episodic engagement, helps us better understand how individuals might engage in contentious politics throughout their lives. While some individuals do become lifelong activists, they constitute a small minority of all participants. Many more disengage after just one period or participate in a more episodic way (what I label *individual abeyance* or *transfer* as outlined in Chapter 1). The trajectory model also provides insight more broadly into the rise and fall of campaigns and movements over time.

What little work there is on contentious political activity over the life course has focused disproportionately on lifelong participants such as Sylvia and James. This focus on persistent participation is a form of selection bias that clouds and distorts our understanding of contentious political activity more generally. When we study only individuals who are still active in movements, we are unable to assess how persistent activists differ from other types of participants as well as from those who never become involved. Casting a wider net and examining different patterns of participation allows us to develop a fuller, more complete understanding of contentious political activity.

In this chapter, I offer a theoretical model with four trajectories of individual participation (outlined in Chapter 1). These trajectories differ in the duration and continuity of engagement over time. In addition, this chapter examines what predicts the trajectory of participation an individual will follow. Who is more likely to become a lifelong activist and who will engage episodically or disengage? Through the use of the Jennings and Stoker panel data, I am able to follow individuals over the course of their lives, from when they were high school seniors in 1965 until 1997, and see them move in and out of participation in contentious politics.

A Theoretical Foundation

How do we understand the different trajectories of participation that individuals can take? Bert Klandermans's theoretical model of movement participation outlined in *The Social Psychology of Protest* (1997) provides an important first step. He outlines three stages of engagement in social movement organizations—initial engagement, sustained participation, and disengagement. Individuals can engage and disengage in two main ways, attitudinally and behaviorally. Attitudinally, a person can feel more or less commitment to a group, and behaviorally she can participate in more or fewer activities. While these two dimensions of engagement and disengagement often overlap, this is not always the case.

Klandermans argues that individuals join movements assuming that the benefits will outweigh the costs. If this expectation is met and interactions with the group prove to be personally satisfying, one develops an affective commitment to the group. If, however, one has disappointing participatory experiences, this weakens commitment and leads to less active participation over time. This can create a self-perpetuating cycle, where less active participation further reduces commitment and precipitates disengagement. Support for a movement also erodes when individuals perceive a higher ratio of costs to benefits, when the grievances no longer seem pressing, or when sympathy for the movement wanes (Klandermans 1997).

These three stages of participation illuminate the processes whereby individuals join and leave specific movement organizations. Yet, as I find in the research presented in this book, many participants engage in this process several times over the course of their lives, joining and leaving a number of different groups or campaigns. I therefore build on Klandermans's three-stage model of participation by extending it from a single organization to patterns of individual participation over the life course.

In addition to Klandermans's theoretical model, there is a small body of work on participation in specific organizations over time as well as follow-up studies of past activists. For example, Sandell (1999) studied the continuity of engagement in the Swedish temperance movement. He was particularly interested in the role of social networks in protecting against movement dropout; individuals tend to leave movements when their close friends do, creating a negative bandwagon effect. Veen and Klandermans (1989) also studied the process of leaving groups, in particular a labor union, and concluded that "exit" behavior is explicable in terms of declining commitment. Both of these studies examine the effect of a particular variable, social networks or commitment, on the continuance of participation in one particular social movement context.

Passy and Giugni (2000) assess these processes on a more general level in their study of why certain activists stay involved in movements. They argue, consistent with the findings presented in Chapter 2, that commitment alone does not predict who remains active over time. Instead, the critical factors that account for continued participation are social networks and the connectedness of an individual's "life-spheres." Specifically, Passy and Giugni argue that the more connected the central life-sphere of an activist to his sphere of political engagement, the more stable his commitment to a movement over time. Conversely, an isolated political sphere is likely to lead to diminished activism or withdrawal. In other words, one's identity and social networks should be connected to one's activism for participation to be sustained over time.

There are also several follow-up studies of New Left activists from the 1960s that aim to assess the effect of social movement participation on the later lives of activists (see, e.g., Fendrich 1993; Jennings and Niemi 1981; McAdam 1989; Whalen and Flacks 1989). These studies follow individual participants over time periods ranging from 4 to 20 years and assess the biographical and personal consequences of participating in social movements. The findings consistently point to the powerful and enduring impact of movement activism, at least for this group of activists. They continue to espouse leftist attitudes, define themselves as liberal or radical in orientation, and remain active in contemporary movements and other forms of political activity. Personally, they are concentrated in the teaching and other helping professions; have lower incomes than their age peers; are more likely than their age peers to have divorced, married later, or remained single; and are more likely than their age peers to have an episodic or nontraditional work history (see Giugni 2004 for a summary of this work).

Beyond these studies, the work on engagement over the life course has been limited. While the research that has been done highlights the importance of certain variables, including identity, commitment, and social ties, and examines the biographical effects of activism, this work only scratches the surface of the ways in which individuals engage in contentious politics and the predictors of continuity of participation.

Our understanding of the processes of engagement in contentious politics can be enriched by examining it through a more general lens of role exiting. All roles are sets of social expectations attached to particular statuses or social positions. Individuals simultaneously perform a variety of roles and move in and out of roles over time. Being a participant in social movements and contentious political activity is one role an individual may perform, and this lens can give us some understanding of the process of engaging in and disengaging from contentious politics.

In her influential work *Becoming an Ex* (1988), Helen Rose Fuchs Ebaugh discusses the concept of role exit, which she describes as the process of disengaging from a role that is central to one's self-identity and reestablishing a new identity in a new role. She posits that the processes whereby individuals leave roles are similar in certain ways, regardless of the substance of the role being left. The duration of the stages of exiting and the events that trigger them may differ; their sequential ordering and the emotions and experiences at each stage, however, are similar.

Erving Goffman also examines role exit in his article *On Cooling the Mark Out* (1952). He argues that disengagement is a mutual process between the individual and other group members. As the person begins to remove herself from the social expectations of a previous role, she emotionally and physically withdraws from other individuals in the group. Like the work of Sandell on social movement engagement, Goffman focuses on the importance of social ties in the exiting process.

Leaving jobs or changing careers can also be seen as processes of role exit. In his study of occupations, Albert O. Hirschman (1970) posits a model of exit and voice that can be very useful for understanding general processes of disengagement. He hypothesizes that the consequences of commitment produce four types of responses. First, individuals can exit and actively destroy the personal link to an organization. Second, they can neglect their commitment and passively allow the relationship or the link with the organization to deteriorate. Third, they can exercise voice, actively and constructively working to improve conditions. Finally, they can display loyalty, passively and optimistically waiting for conditions to improve. High levels of commitment produce constructive responses (voice or loyalty) whereas low levels of commitment produce destructive responses (exit or neglect).

This body of work, including case studies of movement organizations, follow-up studies of activists, and examinations of role exiting, offers a foundation for assessing the predictors of engagement over the life course. I build on this literature in three main ways. First, I use factors that have heretofore only been examined as outcomes of activism to predict the continuity of engagement. For example, in the follow-up studies of activists, Fendrich, McAdam, and others found that those who participated were more politically extreme, had lower incomes, married later, and had less traditional work careers than those who did not. In this analysis, I am able to examine how political ideology, income, marriage, and work history affect activism over time, instead of simply how they are affected *by* activism.

This study also examines the organizational and relational context of engagement. I build on the important insights derived from case studies of specific movements, such as Sandell's work on the Swedish temperance movement and Veen and Klandermans's study of union activists, by looking at individuals in a variety of different groups and causes. I am therefore able to examine the significance of organizational and relational context across a variety of organizations and for individuals who are active in protest but not in organized groups.

Finally, previous studies have emphasized the factors that predict whether or not individuals will remain active over time. However, they do not assess the individuals' patterns or trajectories of engagement. By examining how various predictors are associated with persistent participation, as well as disengagement and intermittent engagement, I am able to assess the extent to which certain factors predict remaining active over time and how these might differ from the predictors of more intermittent and fluctuating engagement.

As individuals move in and out of social movements and contentious political activity, they are engaging and disengaging from the participant role. Through examining case studies of engagement in particular social movement contexts, assessing studies that follow individual activists, and understanding the causes of engaging and disengaging from other roles, we can begin to analyze the process by which individuals move in and out of the role of participant in contentious politics. An understanding of these shifting roles and behaviors can help to account for the variety of trajectories of participation discussed in this book.

Rethinking Activism: Trajectories of Participation

As discussed in the introductory chapter, there are four trajectories that individuals can take once they join a social movement organization (SMO) or participate in an act of protest. First, they can persist in their participation over time, remaining active in protest or the same SMO. Second, they can transfer from one SMO or cause to a different one. In this case, an individual disengages from the first SMO or cause but becomes active in another SMO or cause. Third, they can follow an abeyance trajectory, disengaging from participation but returning to activism later in life. Finally, they can permanently disengage from the SMO and activism altogether. The four biographies that follow provide illustrations of each of these trajectories.[1] They are derived from the interviews conducted for the second half of this book (described in more detail in Chapter 4).

Persistence

Christine had always been an active member of her congregation. In 1980, she attended a women's brunch at her church where Beverly LaHaye, the leader of a conservative Protestant women's organization called Concerned Women for America (CWA), spoke. Christine was inspired by LaHaye and signed up to receive CWA's newsletters. After seven years of receiving the newsletters, Christine began participating in the group and attended a meeting of the local chapter. Her four children were now in school and Christine had more time to dedicate to the cause. At this meeting, the women wrote letters to their congressperson about limiting access to abortion. This was the first time Christine had ever written a letter to a politician or participated in a political activity beyond voting. She attended weekly meetings for 10 years and, in 1997, became the head of CWA in her state, a position she has held to this day. In this capacity, she lobbies government officials, coordinates local chapters within the state, and oversees state-level campaigns. Christine also participates in other conservative groups, such as the Eagle Forum.

Transfer

Henry grew up in Northern California and moved to Santa Monica in 1965 after he graduated from architecture school. He married a year later and raised three daughters in the community. Concerns about funding for local libraries prompted him to join a local neighborhood group in 1971. In 1975, Henry joined another organization that was seeking to restrict the hours that planes could fly into the local airport. He participated in this group for 10 years, with little policy success. Henry attended the initial meeting of the homeowners association in his neighborhood in 1981 and became a board member of the group, a position he held for 20 years. In 2001, Henry and his family moved to Arizona, where he became the chairperson of his local homeowners association there, which lobbies the local government for increased police presence in the community to curb crime.

Abeyance

Anthony's parents had been involved in community activism since the 1940s. Through this work, they met Cesar Chavez and became instrumental in developing a community service organization for Latinos in a small community in California. When he was a child, Anthony worked on the weekends with his parents for the United Farm Workers (UFW), stuffing envelopes or putting stamps on mailers. While at college, Anthony began working part-time in a food-packing plant to pay for school. He was active in the union at his plant and, after graduating, he began working at the plant full-time and became the shop steward for the union. During this period he was not working for the UFW directly but was still active and interested in labor issues. When the grape and lettuce boycotts were initiated, Anthony left his job and went to work at La Paz, the UFW headquarters. After each of these boycott campaigns, he returned to the food-packing plant. This cycle was repeated four times, as Anthony left the plant for periods of six months to two years to work at the UFW headquarters before returning home. During the time he spent away from the UFW headquarters, Anthony did not engage in other types of activism, although he remained interested in labor issues.

Disengagement

John dropped out of his Catholic high school when he was in the eleventh grade. He had been involved in an antiwar student group in high school and, after leaving school, he remained in touch with the teacher who sponsored this group, who was also active in the Catholic Worker (CW) community. In 1969, John began volunteering in the CW community by helping serve meals to the homeless. He moved into the communal home of the group later that year. When describing the group, John remembers these initial months of participation fondly. He says that, at the beginning, the CW community was mostly based on socializing with the other volunteers and was very enjoyable. Over time, as the group aimed to provide meals for larger groups of homeless, John found that it was becoming more of a chore and less of a social gathering. He left the community in 1971, when he moved to a rural area with his wife. He has three children and works as a carpenter. He has lost touch with the other CW participants and has never participated in other social movement groups.

Theoretical Expectations

These biographies illustrate the four trajectories of contentious political engagement outlined in this book. But, who is most likely to participate in each of these ways—who will persist in his involvement and who is more likely to move in and out of activism or disengage over time? In light of the limited research on participation beyond initial engagement, there is little work to directly guide the development of hypotheses to answer these questions. Therefore, I begin by assessing the factors associated with initial engagement discussed in the previous chapter and assess the extent to which those factors also help us to understand later patterns of participation. Chapter 2 showed that ideological factors predispose certain people toward activism. Only those who are biographically available and have certain cultural resources, however, will be able to translate their sympathy into action. While those analyses illuminated the causes of shifting engagement over the life course, they were unable to assess what predicts the pattern, or trajectory, that individual participation will take. The analyses presented in this chapter enable us to do this, giving us a fuller picture of the individual determinants of contentious political activity.

I first examine the role of ideology using four measures: religiosity, political party identification, strength of partisanship, and personal efficacy. As we found in the previous chapter, while having a sympathetic ideology is not sufficient on its own to spark participation, individuals without such an ideology will not be predisposed to engage in contentious action. Ideological factors prime people to participate in contentious politics. Therefore, those who are more religious, leftist, efficacious, and partisan are more likely to initially engage in contentious politics.

Previous research suggests that ideological factors should also matter for patterns of future participation. On the basis of my findings in the previous chapter, however, I do not expect this to be the case. Ideologically sympathetic individuals should be no more likely to persist in their engagement than to follow an abeyance pattern or to disengage—resources and biographical availability should be the critical factors once individuals are involved.

Specifically, I hypothesize that individuals who have more resources are more likely to persist in their engagement over time. In periods of resource scarcity, individuals may have conflicting interests such as working that can reduce their ability to maintain their engagement in activism. Individuals with more resources are more able to persist in their engagement over time because they are less likely to have such periods of resource scarcity. In addition, these resources can help individuals afford things that make activism easier, such as care for children, more flexible work schedules, or transportation to a protest event. Similarly, individuals who are biographically available should be more likely to persist in their participation over time. Those with conflicting role demands, stemming from spouses, children, working, and other constraints, should be more likely to follow an individual abeyance pattern of participation or to disengage.

Following the Trajectories

While the models presented in Chapter 2 examine the factors that give rise to changes in participation over time, they do not directly examine what predicts the trajectory of participation. That is the focus of this chapter, drawing again on the Jennings and Stoker survey. There is, however, an important limitation of this survey for my trajectories model—namely, the survey did not ask about the specific names of the civic and community organizations in which an individual engaged. Therefore, it is not possible to examine the transfer trajectory, or more precisely, it is not possible to distinguish between those who persist in the same group and those who remain active but move from group to group. For example, an individual who initially participated in Greenpeace and then moved to a women's rights group is indistinguishable from one who remained involved with Greenpeace. While the former has persisted in participation over time, she has not persisted in the same organization. Despite this limitation, nevertheless, the analysis is still fruitful, as it allows us to examine the predictors of persistence, abeyance, and disengagement across a wide spectrum of groups and causes. Moreover, we will return to the transfer trajectory in the second half of the book, which is based on the analysis of 60 interviews with participants in four social movement organizations over time.

In order to perform an analysis of trajectories of participation, I coded each person as following one of these three trajectories: persistence, abeyance, or disengagement.[2] I collapse the measures of group and activity participation into a single dichotomous indicator of contentious activity: inactive (0) versus active (1) in each of the four periods. I use these data to create a participation trajectory for each of the respondents who indicated that they had participated in one of the types of activities in at least one of the four periods.

I use a multinomial logistic regression model, because the dependent variable has four categories (never participated, abeyance, persistence, and disengagement, with the latter used as the reference category). In order to create these models, I collapsed the panel data for each person into one data point. Combining the information from all four waves into one data point per person allowed for an examination of the overall characteristics that predict which trajectory of participation an individual will take over time. An individual's trajectory characterizes his engagement over the life course. As the respondent did not have a trajectory until the final period (because it was in process until the final survey), the trajectory is the result of the individual characteristics over the life course.[3] In addition, the models presented here are compared with the panel models presented in Chapter 2, which control for past features in predicting future engagement and make a more definitive statement on causality. The models presented in this chapter, however, extend the panel models by examining the pattern of participation over time, instead of simply whether or not the respondent engaged in the next survey period.

I collapsed the variables as follows. Averages were used for the following variables: family income, level of political knowledge, religiosity, party identification, strength of partisanship, efficacy, number of children at home, and work hours. I used the total years of postsecondary education (from 0 to 7) attained. I also assessed whether or not respondents were ever married over the course of their lives. Information on the coding of trajectories of participation is shown in the Appendix, Table A1.

An Examination of Participation over Time

Figure 6 presents a breakdown of participants by trajectory, excluding those who never participated. The most notable finding from this initial analysis is how relatively few participants follow a persistence trajectory. While past work has tended to focus on this group, it represents only 21 percent of all those who engaged in contentious politics at some point in their lives. In fact, almost twice this number (41%) disengaged after a period of participation, and an additional 38 percent of the respondents were active at one point in their lives but followed an abeyance trajectory of participation. It is clear that there is variety in the trajectories that individuals take in their participation and that the abeyance trajectory, in particular, which has not been theorized in other work, describes a large proportion of activists' experiences over the life course.

In reality, these numbers probably underestimate the proportion of individuals who follow an abeyance trajectory and overestimate the share of persistent activists in the general population. This is because an individual had only to participate once in either a group or an activity during the time period (before 1965, 1966–1973, 1974–1982, and 1983–1997) to be categorized as a

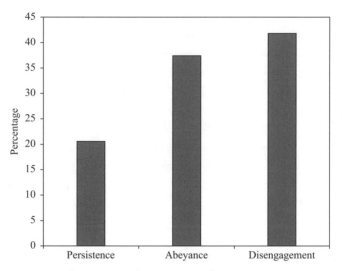

Figure 6 Percentage of participants by trajectory of participation

participant. He did not necessarily need to have participated throughout the time period. Thus, for example, someone who went to one rally in each of 1964, 1969, 1978, and 1995 would be categorized as a participant in each of the four periods and would be coded as persistently engaged. This person, however, might not have engaged in the years between these protests, and so persistence is probably overrepresented and abeyance underrepresented in this study. Even with this likely underrepresentation, however, the abeyance trajectory is still the pathway of almost two-fifths of participants. It is striking, then, that until now research on contentious political participation has not delineated this important trajectory.

What characterizes the individuals who follow each of these trajectories? Table 3 provides the descriptive characteristics of each trajectory group. In general, those who persist or follow an abeyance pattern have more resources than those who disengage. For example, persistent activists tend to have a relatively high income, similar to those who follow an abeyance trajectory but over $5,000 a year more than those who disengage. They also have higher education levels, completing an average of 2.348 years of postsecondary education compared with an average of 1.778 years among individuals who follow an abeyance pattern and 1.300 for those who disengage. Political knowledge is highest among the persisters and those who follow an abeyance pattern; it is lowest among those who disengage.

Table 3 Descriptive background variables by trajectory

	Disengagement		Abeyance		Persistence	
	Mean	*Percent*	*Mean*	*Percent*	*Mean*	*Percent*
Ideology						
Religiosity (0 = No religion, 5 = Weekly)	2.991 (1.084)		3.085 (1.084)		2.858 (1.052)	
Party identification (0 = Strong Democrat, 6 = Strong Republican)	2.787 (1.449)		2.758 (1.620)		2.112 (1.684)	
Strength of partisanship (0 = Weak, 3 = Strong)	1.027 (0.979)		1.151 (1.051)		1.652 (0.982)	
Efficacy (0 = Low, 4 = High)	2.092 (0.540)		2.206 (0.508)		2.271 (0.583)	
Resources						
Income (1997 dollars)	47027.5 (22473.12)		52797.24 (20665.39)		52256.4 (23180.57)	
Postsecondary education (years)	1.300 (1.987)		1.778 (1.910)		2.348 (2.854)	
Political knowledge (0 = Low, 6 = High)	4.303 (1.176)		4.649 (1.091)		4.594 (1.191)	
Biographical availability						
Marital status						
Never married		10.0		10.6		21.7
Has been married		90.0		89.4		78.3
Children						
Never had children		29.2		24.2		26.1
Had children		70.8		75.8		73.9
Work hours (0 = 0, 90 = 90+ hours)	20.103 (12.308)		22.841 (12.247)		23.321 (11.722)	
Control variables						
Gender						
Female		53.4		47.0		47.8
Male		46.6		53.0		52.2
Race						
White		92.0		88.6		78.3
Black		7.1		9.1		17.4
Other		0.9		2.3		4.3
Religion						
Protestant		70.0		67.5		63.3
Catholic		20.4		21.2		25.4
Jewish		4.2		6.6		4.5
Other		0.9		0.5		2.5
None		4.5		4.2		4.3

Ideologically, those who follow an abeyance trajectory are the most reli-gious. Those who disengage are also slightly more religious than those who persist in their participation over the life course. Persisters are more likely to identify as Democrats and to have stronger political partisanship than ei-ther those who follow an abeyance pattern or those who disengage over time. Finally, persisters and those who follow an abeyance trajectory have similar, high levels of efficacy compared to those who disengage.

When looking at biographical availability, it is clear that marriage rates are significantly lower among those who persist in their engagement over time. While approximately 1 in 10 of those who follow an abeyance pattern or disengage over time have never been married, twice that many persisters re-mained unmarried. Interestingly, the percentage of each group that have had children is roughly similar, ranging from 24.2 percent among the abeyance group to 29.2 percent among the disengagers, with the persisters falling in the middle of this range. Finally, those who persist in their engagement work about three hours more per week than those who disengage over time.

Multivariate Findings: Trajectory of Participation

Multinomial Logistic Regression

The multinomial logistic regression model, presented in Table 4, assesses the effect of ideology, resources, and biographical availability on the trajectory of individual participation over the life course. I present the model as a series of logit contrasts between the groups. There are three main findings. First, while ideology predicts engagement in contentious action, it is not related to one's trajectory of participation over time. Second, cultural resources, such as ed-ucation and knowledge, are important predictors of participation trajectory, while financial resources appear to be less important. Finally, biographical availability, particularly marriage and child rearing, predict one's propensity to persist or reengage after a period of inactivity.

Despite the importance of ideology for predicting who will engage initially in contentious political action, as discussed in Chapter 2, it does not appear that ideological factors are related to one's propensity to persist. This is unex-pected, given the stereotype of the lifelong activist, which portrays these in-dividuals as different from other, more sporadic participants because of their strong and deeply held beliefs in their movement's cause (Teske 1997). My analysis, however, shows that political partisanship, religiosity, and feelings of efficacy are not predictors of one's propensity to persist, follow an abeyance

Table 4 Multinomial logistic regression model predicting trajectory of participation

	Never vs. disengage	Abeyance vs. disengage	Persist vs. disengage
Intercept	6.814***	−6.101*	−7.459
	(1.695)	(2.471)	(5.420)
Ideology			
Religiosity	−0.332***	0.142	−0.042
	(0.084)	(0.102)	(0.248)
Party identification	0.119	0.090	0.239
	(0.078)	(0.093)	(0.220)
Strength of partisanship	0.087	0.212	0.719*
	(0.115)	(0.137)	(0.322)
Efficacy	−0.688***	0.199	0.381
	(0.163)	(0.209)	(0.467)
Resources			
Income (logged)	−0.975*	0.318	0.073
	(0.391)	(0.559)	(1.216)
Postsecondary education	−0.069	0.091*	0.185*
	(0.046)	(0.045)	(0.089)
Political knowledge	−0.309***	0.235*	0.171
	(0.079)	(0.103)	(0.240)
Biographical availability			
Married	−0.064	−0.343	−1.830*
	(0.301)	(0.380)	(0.819)
Children	0.095	−0.559*	−1.297*
	(0.209)	(0.280)	(0.758)
Work hours	−0.006	0.011	0.013
	(0.019)	(0.026)	(0.065)
Work hours squared	0.001	0.001	0.001
	(0.001)	(0.001)	(0.001)
Controls			
Gender	0.656***	0.082	0.219
	(0.188)	(0.227)	(0.517)
White (omitted category)			
Black	−0.853*	0.360	1.394
	(0.389)	(0.386)	(0.767)
Other minority group	0.546	0.826	1.260
	(0.695)	(0.734)	(1.154)
Protestant (omitted category)			
Catholic	0.468*	−0.017	1.067
	(0.201)	(0.260)	(0.613)
Jewish or other religion	−0.257	0.195	1.992*
	(0.444)	(0.422)	(0.726)

NOTE: Numbers in parentheses are standard deviations.

*$p < 0.05$

**$p < 0.01$

***$p < 0.001$

pattern of participation, or disengage over time; they are predictors only of initial participation. It is possible that there is a base level of ideological predisposition or commitment required in order to make the initial decision to join a social movement, but once that hurdle has been surmounted, ideological differences among participants become less important for predicting continued engagement.

The lack of significance of religion in predicting an individual's pattern or trajectory of participation is notable. Religion has always played a somewhat conflicting role in fostering contentious political activity. It has played a critical role in sustaining many past campaigns, particularly the civil rights movement, which was famously cultivated within African American churches (McAdam 1999). But religion is often associated with conservative beliefs (Luker 1984; Page and Clelland 1978), and many religious institutions focus on conformity and obedience, which can suppress participation (Ellison and Sherkat 1993). So while some religious institutions might be supporting activism, others clearly are not.

Beyond the level of religiosity, however, religious denomination is significant, as illuminated by the significance of the religion control variable. Individuals who identified themselves as Jewish or as members of other non-Christian religions were more likely than Protestants (the reference category) to persist in their participation over time. This finding supports the work of Snow and Oliver (1993), who show that Jews, because of their historical experiences and ethnic origins, were more likely to have participated in the protests of the 1960s. Other research on activism in later time periods supports this finding (Sherkat and Blocker 1993).

It is also interesting to note that efficacy is not a significant predictor of persistent engagement. While the analyses presented in Chapter 2 showed that efficacy is strongly related to one's propensity to have ever engaged in contentious political action, it is not significantly related to persisting in that participation. One perspective on social movements suggests that individual participation in collective action is partly a function of weighing the costs and benefits of engagement (Zald and McCarthy 1987). From this perspective, those who feel that they are most able to affect the world around them should be most likely to engage and persist in this type of collective action, yet this does not appear to be the case.

While ideological factors as a whole are not significant predictors of participatory trajectories, there is one notable exception—strong partisans are more likely to persist over time. Indeed, strong partisans are more than four times as likely to persist in their participation as weak partisans. Thus, it is not whether you are Republican or Democrat but how strongly you identify with one party or the other that influences your propensity to persist in participation over the life course. Despite the significance of this variable, while ideological factors may predispose certain individuals to initially engage, they are generally not strong predictors of what happens to individuals after they initially participate in contentious political action.

Turning now to the role of cultural resources, education and knowledge are important for protecting against disengagement from protest. Individuals with more education are less likely to disengage over time and are more likely to either persist or follow an abeyance trajectory. In fact, individuals who have a four-year college degree are twice as likely to persist and 1.44 times more likely to follow an abeyance trajectory, as opposed to disengage, than those who have only a high school diploma. Education is partly correlated with job status, which may explain its significance in predicting either persistent engagement or reengagement after a lull in participation. Jobs that require more education often involve a higher degree of autonomy and a flexible schedule, which could enable persistent engagement or reengagement.

Individuals who have more political knowledge are also more likely to follow an abeyance pattern of participation instead of disengaging permanently; answering two additional questions correctly on the political knowledge test increases one's chances of following an abeyance trajectory by a factor of 1.60. It is interesting to note, however, that political knowledge is not associated with persistent participation. This could be because returning to activism after a lull requires paying attention to current affairs and social issues. Only if individuals follow the media and issues in their community will they know about ways to return to engagement after a period of inactivity. For individuals who persist in action continuously, such general political knowledge is not necessary as they can learn about events and campaigns through the groups in which they are involved.

Income is not a significant predictor of engagement over time. As discussed in Chapter 2, the role of income in predicting involvement in traditional political activity and social movements is fairly strong and consistent in past work (Leighley and Nagler 1992; Rosenstone and Hansen 1993; Verba et al. 1995). The lack of significance of this variable in this analysis is, therefore, notable. However, despite the nonsignificance of this variable, resources as a whole are still important predictors of engagement over time; it is simply that cultural resources matter more than financial ones. The delineation of the different types of resources helps to illuminate how knowledge and education play a role independent of income in predicting one's trajectory of participation.

Finally, the results reinforce the importance of biographical factors in predicting one's trajectory over the life course. Individuals who have been married, for example, are more likely to disengage over time instead of persisting. In fact, a person who has been married at any point in time is over six times more likely to disengage from participation. This finding supports the results presented in Chapter 2, that while there is a negative relationship between marriage and political engagement, it is the transition to marriage that in fact suppresses participation. Individuals who are single are more likely to be involved in protest, and those people who remain single over the life course remain relatively more likely to engage. If and when individuals marry, they decrease their chances of participating. But if these same people who were married later separate, divorce, or are widowed, they often return to participation.

Thus, while marriage suppresses participation, it is a change in one's marital status, from single to married or married to single, that shifts the propensity to engage in contentious politics. In the model presented here, examining the role of whether or not one has ever been married (regardless of current marital status), I show that individuals who have been married are also much less likely to persist in their participation. Thus marriage suppresses both one's likelihood of participating and one's propensity to persist in engagement over time.

In addition, the longitudinal panel model shows that having children at any point in the life course makes individuals more likely to disengage over time. Individuals who have children are almost twice as likely to disengage than follow an abeyance trajectory and four times more likely to disengage than persist in their participation over time. This finding also illuminates the results of Chapter 2, where I showed that there is a positive relationship between child rearing and participation: having children increases one's likelihood of participating in contentious politics. Thus, while having children makes one more likely to engage at some point, individuals who have children are less able to sustain their participation over time.

Discussion and Conclusion

In this chapter, I consider a typology of trajectories of participation in social movements and contentious politics. Previous work has tended to focus on individuals who either join a social movement and persist in that engagement over their lives or disengage after one period of activism. My findings, however, show that approximately two-fifths of those who have participated in contentious politics at one point in their lives have experienced abeyance trajectories, going through periods of activism followed by lulls and then re-engagement. This supports a broader conceptualization of engagement as following one of several possible trajectories and helps us recognize the waves of participation in which many activists engage.

Through an assessment of initial engagement and trajectory of participation over time, I show that predictors of initial and sustained engagement are not identical. By examining individuals over the course of their lives, we are able to assess both the factors that predict who will engage and those that will keep individuals active over time. Many factors that increase one's propensity to initially engage are not associated with sustained engagement. For example, ideological factors are important predictors of ever engaging in contentious politics; individuals who are more religious and efficacious, as well as on the political left, are more likely to have ever engaged. Ideological factors, however, are not significant predictors of shifting involvement or trajectory of participation over time. In fact, the only ideological factor found to have an effect on one's trajectory of participation is the strength of one's partisanship. Religion, left-right ideology (measured as partisanship), and efficacy are not predictors of engagement over time. These factors seem to work to initially pull individuals into participation but then have little influence on subsequent patterns of participation after that initial engagement.

Resources are important predictors of both whether or not one ever engages and one's trajectory of participation over time. Those with higher levels of education and knowledge are more likely to have ever engaged and to either persist or follow an abeyance pattern over time, instead of disengaging permanently after a period of participation. These cultural resources both prime individuals to participate and keep them active over time. The financial resource of income, however, is not a significant predictor either of ever having engaged or of one's trajectory of participation over time in these models.

Finally, biographical changes are significant and important predictors of whether or not individuals engage in contentious politics, their shifting participation over time, and their trajectory of engagement. For example, individuals who are married are less likely to have ever participated in contentious politics (as compared with those who remained single or who separated, divorced, or were widowed); individuals are likely to shift out of engagement when they marry; and individuals who are married are more likely to follow a disengagement trajectory of participation over time, never returning to activism. Child rearing also has an interesting relationship with engagement in social movements and protest. Individuals who have children are more likely to have ever engaged. However, individuals who have children are also more likely to follow a disengagement trajectory of participation over time, rather than persisting or following an abeyance pattern. This suggests that, while individuals may be pulled into social movements by having children, the time demands of child rearing limit the ability of parents to maintain their participation over time. Finally, number of hours worked has a curvilinear relationship with engagement, in that individuals who either do not work at all or work more than full-time are less likely to have ever engaged in contentious politics than those who work full-time. Working, however, is not significantly associated with one's trajectory of participation over time.

While the findings from this and the previous chapter can be generalized, as they are based on a large, nationally representative sample, several important questions remain unanswered. First, we cannot examine the transfer trajectory of participation with the panel data. As respondents were not asked the specific names of groups, it is not possible to determine whether individuals persisted in the same group or remained active but moved from group to group. Second, central to my model is the link between the organizational context and individual-level factors more generally. Individuals make decisions to join social movement organizations or participate in protest events within an organizational and relational context. It is clear that the experience of participating in a small, egalitarian group that involves high levels of interaction among members is quite different from the experience of engaging in a large, hierarchical group that involves little contact between participants. This likely has implications for individual participation patterns over time. I will turn to a more detailed analysis of how organizational and social-psychological factors affect participation in the second half of the book.

4 Social, Political, and Organizational
Context of Participation

NOT ALL PARTICIPATION IS EQUIVALENT. The experience and meaning of engaging in contentious politics depend on the organizational and relational context in which this engagement occurs. For example, a person who joins a local beach cleanup group and walks the shores with friends every weekend has a very different experience of engagement than one who is a member of a large national group such as the Sierra Club and rarely interacts with other group members. Individuals will experience participation differently, in part because of the organizational context in which it occurs. This context, in turn, has important implications for the patterns of participation over time—indeed, the organizational context is just as critical as the individual-level characteristics analyzed in the previous two chapters, if not more so, for shaping individuals' engagement. The role of organizational and relational context is captured in the overall model presented in Chapter 1 (see Figure 1): once individuals begin to participate in contentious politics, their participation necessarily occurs within an organizational and relational context. This context shapes the identities that individuals develop and the social ties they foster in the course of participation, which in turn influences the length and continuity of the individuals' participation over time—their trajectory of participation. These relationships are the focus of the second part of this book, and in order to examine them in more detail, I move from the large-scale panel data analysis to a more detailed comparative case studies approach.

Many case studies examine individual social movement organizations and the recruitment of individuals to those organizations (e.g., Blee 2002; Ginsburg 1998; Klatch 1999; Whittier 1995). However, the limited amount of comparative work makes it difficult to draw any general conclusions about the exact role of the social, political, and organizational context. For example, how can we tell how the experience of engagement in a large hierarchical group differs from participation in a small communal organization? While we have case studies of each type of group, there are always many other differences between the groups that make it difficult to compare them. For this reason, it is challenging to pinpoint the effect of contextual factors on the duration and continuity of individual participation. In order to enrich these past case studies and the findings of my quantitative data analysis, I selected four social movement organizations and conducted intensive life-history interviews with past participants in each of these groups. In this chapter, I describe the four organizations and explore the ways in which their contexts differ. My purpose is to give some background information on the organizations and set the stage for the more detailed analyses presented in Chapters 5 and 6.

Comparison of the four organizations adds to the earlier quantitative analysis in three main ways. First, it allows for an assessment of how organizational structure, particularly issue scope, intensity of interaction, and degree of hierarchy within the group, shapes an individual's trajectory of participation. Second, interviews of movement participants allow for an examination of social-psychological factors, such as social ties and identity, that have been important in past work in predicting initial engagement and participation over time. Measures for these factors were not included in the Jennings and Stoker survey instrument. Finally, I am able to assess the key difference between the transfer trajectory and the abeyance and persistence trajectories, which could not be assessed with the Jennings and Stoker panel survey used in Chapters 2 and 3.[1] A closer examination of the transfer trajectory also gives greater insight into the variety of ways in which individuals can engage in contentious politics over the life course.

I interviewed past participants from a sample of four social movement organizations (SMOs) with the purpose of illuminating their engagement and tracing their participation trajectories; for example, did they remain in their SMO, leave their SMO for another SMO, leave their SMO and participation for a time and later return, or leave their SMO and participation permanently? The four groups were intentionally chosen so as to vary in terms of degree of hierarchy, level and intensity of social interaction, and issue scope.

The Role of Organizational Context

The organizational context in which a person engages shapes his experience of participation. While there has been a large body of research on the effects of participation in civil society organizations, it is clear that not all organizations have the same impact on individuals or larger democratic systems (Warren 2001). The organizational structure has significant effects on the social ties and identities that participants create in the course of engagement. I examine two fundamental features of organizational context in this project: the organization's degree of hierarchy and its issue scope. Figure 7 shows how the four groups differ on these two dimensions.

Degree of Hierarchy

Groups differ in terms of their degree of hierarchy, which we can conceptualize as varying along a continuum from very hierarchical to very egalitarian. Hierarchical organizations are more formalized and centralized than egalitarian groups, that is, they tend to have an explicit written scheme of organization, a clear division of labor, and a strong central leadership that directs the subgroupings. In theory, formalization and centralization can vary independently; in practice, they tend to be strongly correlated. An SMO high in one respect is likely to be high in the other, and vice versa (Gamson 1990; Lofland 1996).[2]

In larger, more hierarchical organizations, decision making tends to be highly centralized (Knoke 1981; Steers 1977). As a consequence, rank-and-file

	HIERARCHY	
	← Less	More →
Multi-issue	Catholic Worker community	Concerned Women for America
ISSUE SCOPE		
Single-issue	Homeowners Association (NIMBY group)	United Farm Workers

Figure 7 Sample of social movement organizations

members have less influence over group decisions, including group activities and overall direction. This lack of influence can lower members' commitment to the organization and increase their sense of detachment and alienation (Knoke 1981). This suggests that individuals are less likely to actively persist in hierarchical groups over time. In smaller or less hierarchical organizations, individuals may have more of an impact on collective decision making (Steers 1977). Collective decision making often plays an important role in motivating the continuing commitment of movement participants over time (Hirsch 1990) and may increase feelings of efficacy, attachment, and satisfaction within the group. Even if participants are unhappy with outcomes, they may still feel bound by them if they are a part of the decision-making process (Rosenthal and Schwartz 1989). For these reasons, individuals may be more likely to remain active in less hierarchical social movement organizations over time.

Groups also differ in the extent to which they involve intensive interaction among their members. Hierarchical groups are less likely to have this type of interaction, although this is not always the case. Groups with high levels of interaction tend to create bonds of solidarity by enmeshing members in a set of overlapping and interlocking relationships. Such relationships produce strong and reciprocal interpersonal ties, including intensive friendships among group members, which can generate powerful incentives for continued participation over time (Knoke 1981).[3]

One way to offset the negative effects of a large group and hierarchical structure on member commitment and participation is to have a federated organizational structure. Federated groups involve a centralized structure, often at a national or state level, and smaller subgroups, often at the community or local level. Large national movement organizations without such a structure are composed of isolated constituents who typically have little contact with the organization or with each other, making it difficult for them to develop strong attachments to the organization or other members (McCarthy and Zald 1977). Federated structures can counter some of the negative effects of group hierarchy, effectively creating smaller organizations within a larger one. However, empirical studies, such as Barkan et al.'s (1993) work on Bread for the World, find that being a member of a local group plays only a small role in increasing commitment over time. The roles of size, level of hierarchy, and federated structure need to be assessed in more detail in additional empirical studies, and this book begins to address this gap.

Issue Scope (Single- and Multi-issue Groups)

Social movement organizations also differ in the extent to which they focus on a specific issue or on a set of interconnected issues. Many social movements are based on ideologies that join together a number of specific beliefs. In the present study, the Catholic Workers and Concerned Women for America are examples of groups that offer holistic ideologies of social justice and conservative Protestant Christianity, respectively.[4] The organizations work to tie together specific issues, such as antiwar work and ending homelessness in the case of the Catholic Workers, with an overarching ideology.

Not all social movements, however, are organized around a wide range of interconnected issues and beliefs. There are many single-issue movements where there is no active, formal effort on the part of leaders or members to link their issue with other issues. Group members often express very high levels of commitment to these causes, but the organization does not present them as connected to other issues. In this study, the United Farm Workers and the Homeowners Association are examples of single-issue groups that do not directly tie their respective issues to a larger, overarching ideology. For example, the United Farm Workers promotes the rights of farm workers, but tends not to get involved in other issues of the political left, such as antiwar mobilization or women's rights.

In this analysis I compare what I label "multi-issue" groups with "single-issue" groups and groups that vary in their degree of hierarchy. These two dimensions of organizational context are significant because they affect the types of ties and identities participants develop in the course of their engagement. In turn, these identities and ties affect the length and continuity of an individual's participation.

Logic of Movement Organization Selection

I have selected groups that represent the four possible combinations of these two variables (high and low hierarchy and multi- and single-issue scope). Figure 7 lists the groups in this analysis and their organizational characteristics. I selected 15 past participants from each of the four groups for a total of 60 interviews. The individuals I selected participated either in 1970 (United Farm Workers and Catholic Workers) or in 1980 (Concerned Women for America and the Homeowners Association), allowing me to inquire about their participation since that time. The following section gives an overview of each of these four groups.

Four Organizational Contexts

A Catholic Worker Group (Low Hierarchy, Multi-issue)

The Catholic Worker (CW) movement was founded in 1933 by Dorothy Day, a journalist who was received into the Catholic Church in 1927. The organization is best known for its "houses of hospitality" for the homeless, located in low-income urban areas. In 2007, there were 185 such communities (www .catholicworker.org). In addition, the group works in support of labor issues, human rights, disarmament, and the development of a nonviolent culture. The CW model stresses voluntary poverty and is founded on "sacrifice, worship, and a sense of reverence" (Dorothy Day, quoted in Piehl 1982).

A notable feature of the group and the loose network of affiliated CW communities is that they are highly unstructured: each community is autonomous, there is no board of directors or system of governance, and all decisions at the local level are made by consensus (Coy 2001, 78). In addition, since Dorothy Day's death in 1980 there has been no central leader. Despite the lack of official leadership, however, there is communication between the local CW communities; many members travel from one CW house to another over time and there is a CW newsletter that ties the communities together and helps them share information and strategies.

The CW community I examine in this study is located in a large midwestern city in the United States and was founded in the late 1960s. This CW community worked on two core sets of issues that were strongly connected and mutually reinforcing. First, the group was centrally concerned with resisting the Vietnam War and was organized on the basis of networks formed through the antiwar work of the founders (including protesting and observant objections). Second, the group worked on community issues, particularly the issues of poverty and homelessness. This group observed the Catholic Worker principle, articulated by Arnold, a 57-year-old librarian, that you "don't abstract yourself from all aspects of the world . . . or from social problems." Therefore, as another participant explained, the group worked by "rolling up [their] sleeves and getting involved in social change."[5] This community was fairly typical of CW groups at the time in terms of its focus on the homeless and on resisting war.

Many of the original members of this CW community met while they were living in a suburb. They were interested in the Catholic Peace Movement and formed a reading group in a Catholic church in 1968 to learn about racism, poverty, and war. In light of the political context around them, including the escalating resistance to the war in Vietnam, these original members felt that they were not doing enough to deal with these issues directly. Patricia, a laboratory technician in an environmental research institute, told me that the group sought to address war, racism, and homelessness by "giv[ing] some kind of direct and hands-on support . . . to the community." Two of the founding members of the community were priests who had been arrested the previous year for giving an antiwar sermon in a cathedral and for pacifist antiwar protest in Washington, DC, resulting in their excommunication from the church. One of these priests, who continued to engage in social justice work after his excommunication and was later readmitted to the priesthood, told me that a small group of people wanted to move into a poor area of the city to "live the life that [they] were talking about," serving the poor and helping build community.

This call to action was met with overwhelming support from those involved in the reading group, and a small, strongly committed group of people bought homes in a poor, urban community in 1965—what Margaret, a 63-year-old nurse, described as the "catch-all significantly nonblack poor neighborhood" of the city. They sought not only to change the community around them but also to live intentionally in a community themselves within the houses. The initial group consisted of three households. Single families resided in two of the houses, while the third was referred to as the "hippy house"—a large, dilapidated building with 15 rooms occupied by the single residents. Once the initial group were living in the communal homes, more individuals, including students from universities and high schools together with other people in the area, came to join the community.

The establishment of the CW community fundamentally altered the neighborhood around the communal homes. Many other like-minded individuals, liberal and activist in orientation, moved to the area. Jesuit volunteers, for example, came to live in a neighboring house and participated in some of the group's activities. These individuals often remained in the area after they had completed a year of service, partly because of the sense of community created by the CW group, which transformed the neighborhood as a whole.

Soon after the group moved into the initial houses, they began holding a potluck dinner every Friday in a church basement. After a few weeks they invited the homeless to come to the dinners. One member notes that initially there were more CWs than homeless at dinner and the atmosphere was highly social. Over time, however, more and more homeless came, and the group began offering meals on more nights through a variety of churches in the area. This program expanded to nightly meals around the neighborhood and continues to this day, serving approximately 350 people per night. In addition, the members began to use the communal houses in which they lived to provide hospitality to the homeless. The meals program and the hospitality houses were the staple programs of this group and are good examples of how the group sought to expand to meet the changing needs of their community.

The CW community was composed of dense social networks and ties and the participants spent a lot of time socializing. A woman who was a resident of the area and joined the group in her early twenties told me, "We often sat in each other's kitchens smoking cigarettes and drinking coffee. That was our main form of recreation. It was wonderful because we talked long into the night and enjoyed each other's company." These networks were strengthened not only by their shared volunteer work with the homeless and in antiwar activities but also by the fact that they lived together and often worked in similar paid employment.[6] There were two main types of employment in the group. Some individuals worked in low-skill, low-pay jobs that they considered a necessary evil to support themselves, the communal household, and the programs they ran, all of which were funded with their own money. These jobs included working as nursing home aides, as warehouse staff, or in stores. The majority of those in the community, however, worked in social justice–related jobs in the neighborhood, as adult education teachers, priests, or community development workers, among others.

Much like the national organization, the group was loosely structured and had no formalized or centralized leadership. Individuals were encouraged either to participate in the core programs of the group, the antiwar work and the meals for the homeless, or to start their own projects. These other projects included a food cooperative, a community bail fund, an antiwar comic book, a community farm, a coffeehouse for teenagers in a church basement, and a free medical clinic. Those in the CW community were not required to participate in any activities in order to stay in the house, and they only paid a small amount, $25 per week, to sustain the house. Yet all of the individuals I interviewed participated actively while they lived there and donated a great deal of time and energy to these programs, ranging from a low of 10 hours a week to a high of 60 or more hours a week.

Religion played an interesting role in the community. Notably, not all of the CWs were conventionally religious and not all those who were religious were Catholic. Jeremy, who now owns a used book store, explains:

By no means all of us, but some of us had strong Catholic backgrounds. And, for the rest of the group, there was a strong feeling that you could understand where they were coming from without having a conversation about it. There was a feeling of shared history even though we didn't necessarily come from the same neighborhoods or know each other before. We still knew where people were coming from intellectually and spiritually and we trusted people.

Catholicism did not directly inform the actions of the group, but the values associated with the CW ideology, such as serving others, working with the poor, and pacifism, were important for the group as a whole and worked as the "glue that bound [them] together."[7] Sean, who now works as a housing judge in the city, told me that "although everyone wasn't Catholic by any means, it was the kind of the thing that brought us together. A lot of the people didn't go to mass or anything like that. But it was the underlying values." These values, whether learned through religious upbringing or not, practiced or not, associated with organized religion or not, sustained and drove the work done by the CW group members.

Slowly, over time, most individuals left this CW community. Throughout the 1980s and early 1990s, the gentrification of the surrounding neighborhood, as well as life-cycle changes for individuals (such as marriage and having children), led many of the participants to leave the communal houses. Some of the participants moved out and most set up single-family homes in the area. Others stayed in the communal homes while their roommates moved out, leaving them with ownership of the houses. And some CWs left the area and moved away.

In summary, the CW community was egalitarian in orientation. There were no leaders and decisions were made by consensus. The group involved high levels of intensive interaction among members, often resulting in close friendships and romantic partnering.[8] Finally, the group had a broad ideological scope. While many were initially drawn to the group because of its work resisting the Vietnam War, the group worked on a multitude of issues and most participants became actively involved in a variety of causes. The ideology of the group explicitly tied multiple issues, such as helping the homeless, pacifism, and community outreach, to an overarching ideology of social justice. I interviewed 15 individuals who were actively involved in the community in 1970. For information on the sampling procedure, see the Appendix; for demographic information on my sample, see Table 5.

Table 5 Sample characteristics by group

	Catholic Workers	Concerned Women for America	United Farm Workers	Homeowners Association	Total (four groups)	National sample (1960 census)
Gender						
Female	40% (6)	100% (15)	40% (6)	73% (11)	65% (38)	48%
Education						
Less than high school	7% (1)	—	—	—	2% (1)	9%
High school graduate	7% (1)	27% (4)	7% (1)	20% (3)	15% (9)	18%
Some college	—	20% (3)	13% (2)	—	8% (5)	18%
College degree	33% (5)	33% (5)	40% (6)	40% (6)	37% (22)	35%
Advanced degree	53% (8)	20% (3)	40% (6)	40% (6)	38% (23)	20%
Occupation						
Homemaker	—	66% (10)	—	27% (4)	23% (14)	
Manual labor	7% (1)	—	7% (1)	—	3% (2)	
Service	7% (1)	—	—	7% (1)	3% (2)	
Professional	87% (13)	33% (5)	93% (14)	66% (10)	70% (42)	
Marital status						
Single	30% (3)	—	13%(2)	7% (1)	10% (6)	10%
Married	53% (8)	73% (11)	73% (11)	80% (12)	70% (42)	67%
Divorced/separated	27% (4)	—	13% (2)	13% (2)	13% (8)	15%
Widowed	—	27% (4)	—	—	7% (4)	8%

Has children	66% (10)	100% (15)	87% (13)	60% (9)	78% (47)	79%
Religion						
None	33% (5)	—	—	33% (5)	17% (10)	3%
Catholic	60% (9)	—	80% (12)	7% (1)	37% (22)	21%
Mainline Protestant	7% (1)	27% (4)	7% (1)	40% (6)	20% (12)	70%[a]
Evangelical Protestant	—	73% (11)	13% (2)	7% (1)	23% (14)	
Jewish	—	—	—	13% (2)	3% (2)	3%
Other	—	—	—	—	—	1%
Religiosity						
Never attends	33% (5)	—	—	40% (6)	18% (11)	10%
Attends less than two times a month	20% (3)	53% (8)	73% (11)	27% (4)	42% (25)	33%
Attends three to four times a month	33% (5)	40% (6)	13% (2)	33% (5)	30% (18)	35%
Attends more than weekly	20% (3)	7% (1)	13% (2)	—	10% (6)	22%
Mean Age						
At time of interview[b]	61.87	63.33	61.00	64.20	62.60	61.00
Range	(53–81)	(50–81)	(48–73)	(46–80)	(46–81)	
In 1970 or 1980[c]	25.87	37.33	25.00	38.20	31.60	

[a]Mainline and evangelical Protestants are not distinguishable in the national sample.

[b]Interviews were conducted in 2005.

[c]The Catholic Workers and the United Farm Workers were sampled from 1970 and Concerned Women for America and the Homeowners Association were sampled from 1980.

Concerned Women for America (High Hierarchy, Multi-issue)

Concerned Women for America (CWA) is a multi-issue women's group founded by Beverly LaHaye. LaHaye heard Betty Friedan (the founder of the National Organization for Women) interviewed on the radio and was angry that NOW purported to speak for all women. She founded CWA as a response to "protect and promote biblical values among all citizens" and to "reverse the decline in moral values of our nation." This organization is "socially conservative" and "deeply religious," seeing "the traditional heterosexual family as the core of society" (Schreiber 2002).

CWA is one of seven major Christian Right organizations founded in what Moen (1992) calls the expansionist period of the Christian Right in the United States, from 1979 to 1984.[9] All of these groups work on issues relating to traditional conservative Protestant values and the expression of these values in American politics. CWA has considerable support among Christians. Bendyna and colleagues (2001) find that 78 percent of evangelical Protestants, 54 percent of mainline Protestants, and 67 percent of Catholics support the work of CWA. This level of support is higher than the support for three other large religious Right organizations about which they asked questions: the Christian Coalition, the Moral Majority, and Operation Rescue (57).

CWA is unique among organizations of the religious Right in a number of ways. First, it is the only Christian Right organization founded and led by a woman, and it has a predominantly female membership. In addition, while the other groups in this movement were founded in Washington and have little interaction with their grassroots base, CWA has a strong grassroots component and, in fact, did not move its head office to Washington until 1985.[10] Finally, CWA remained explicitly religious while other groups in this movement became more secular over time, toning down their religious rhetoric (Moen 1992). CWA has had significant political impact and has been called a "key Christian-Right organization of the post-Reagan era" (Moen 1992, 53).

CWA has six core issue areas on which its members work. First, they are concerned with education, including sex education in schools and school prayer. Second, they work on religious freedom campaigns, mostly based on protecting Protestant Christian beliefs and practices from perceived infringement from the state. Third, they are concerned with protecting a traditional definition of marriage and the family, particularly working against the legalization of gay marriage. Fourth, they organize around pro-life issues. These campaigns originally concentrated on limiting access to abortion but now include efforts to combat euthanasia and stem-cell research. Fifth, they attempt to limit access to pornography and control the use of violent and sexual content in the media. Finally, they work on issues of "national sovereignty," which they see as encroached upon by the United Nations (www.cwfa.org).

CWA was founded in San Diego in 1979. Believing that "the feminist's anti-God, anti-family rhetoric didn't represent her interests" or those "of the vast majority of women," Beverly LaHaye organized a small circle of friends to discuss opposition to the "feminist agenda," particularly the Equal Rights Amendment (Moen 1992). The small group organized an anti-ERA rally at a local theater in San Diego that attracted 1,200 women. After this rally, the women began organizing local prayer action chapters. These prayer action chapters are the basis of CWA, and the organization as a whole uses the "power of prayer" as one of their primary social movement tactics.[11] As Sally, a 51-year-old stay-at-home mother, told me:

> We are the one organization, of all the public policy organizations, that really puts a large emphasis on prayer. The way I look at it, that is a secret weapon that we have that a lot of organizations, even though they might define themselves as Christian and probably do pray, but they don't encourage it as a basis of what they do. And that to me is probably the defining thing that separates us from other groups.

The organization is highly centralized but has a federated structure. Each of the prayer action chapters across the country, which numbered just under 2,000 by the end of the 1980s, has a leader who reports to the state leadership. At the state level, CWA lobbies legislatures and reports to the national head office. The national head office, which moved from San Diego to Washington, DC, in 1985, produces materials such as a monthly newsletter, holds an annual convention, gives advice and support to the state leaders, and organizes and mobilizes new prayer action chapters across the country.

In 2002, the group had approximately 500,000 members (Schreiber 2002), an annual budget of $6 million, and 30 full-time staff (Rohlinger 2002). CWA is primarily funded in two ways. First, members pay a $25 annual fee for which they receive the monthly periodical containing feature stories on locally active women, updates on litigation and group activities, and solicited articles from leading conservatives on issues such as abortion and gay marriage. Second, some large corporations, including Pepsico, Avon, Levi

Strauss, Subaru, and American Express, have matched employee contributions to CWA (Moen 1992).

Although some men work at the national office, CWA is composed almost exclusively of women at the grassroots. The women involved are all Christian, with most participating in Evangelical churches and/or considering themselves to be "born again" Christians. The remaining women are from mainline Protestant churches. All women interviewed participate actively in their churches, attending at least once a week, with many doing so more often. Although some of the women I interviewed work outside of the home, the majority of the women are stay-at-home mothers and all are married with children.

Most of the women I interviewed were recruited to the group through personal contact either with the leader, Beverly LaHaye, or with one of the women from the head office. These women were asked by the recruiters to attend meetings in their area, start a prayer action chapter, or start a state chapter.[12] One woman describes how she originally got involved in CWA:

> I started as the director in the [city where I live]. We had lived in [another city] and my husband sold his business and we moved down here. A woman who was working with Mrs. LaHaye as her special assistant called and asked if they could hold a meeting in my home and invite people in the area who might be interested in starting a steering committee here. So, we did that and I came on as director. So, that is how I started as a volunteer.

It is remarkable, given the size of the group, that so many of the participants were personally recruited by LaHaye or her direct associates. However, this reemphasizes the commitment of the leadership of CWA to grassroots organizing and the role of prayer action chapters as the heart of CWA. This personal recruitment was the impetus for the initial mobilization of most group members.

In summary, CWA is a hierarchical organization. It has a clearly delineated leadership and organizational hierarchy flowing from the national head office down to local prayer action chapters. Its ideological scope is broad: the organization explicitly ties multiple issues, such as opposition to abortion, gay marriage, and stem-cell research, together under the broader ideology of conservative Protestant Christianity. I interviewed 15 members active in this group in 1980 (for information on sampling, see the Appendix; for information on the demographic profile of this group, see Table 5).

United Farm Workers (High Hierarchy, Single-issue)

Immigrant and migrant farm laborers in California and elsewhere have long been a group subject to poor and unsafe working conditions. In order to address the problems faced by this group, Cesar Chavez founded the National Farm Workers Association (NFWA) in 1962 to help farm workers through programs aimed at improving their economic security and developing their communities. By the summer of 1965, the NFWA had over 500 active members and began expanding beyond economic benefits programs (such as a credit union and cooperative buying for farm workers) to unionization.

Concurrently, in 1965, an active group of Filipino work crews in the Agricultural Workers Organizing Committee (AWOC) launched a series of wage strikes in the Coachella Valley and Delano areas. A week later, on September 16, the NFWA joined the AWOC picket lines (Dunne 1967; London and Anderson 1970). In 1966, the mostly Latino NFWA merged with the Filipino AWOC to create the United Farm Workers, led by Cesar Chavez. This union works to achieve collective-bargaining rights for US farm workers. Through these bargaining rights, the UFW seeks to give workers dignity, improve wages, and ameliorate working and safety conditions for migrant farm laborers (www.ufw.com).

Initially the UFW's strikes were unsuccessful. Police intimidation, the replacement of workers by playing on ethnic rivalries, and the use of scab workers weakened the actions of the union (Dunne 1967; London and Anderson 1970; Matthiessen 1969). However, outside support from religious groups and organized labor came to the union's aid and provided a stable resource base. The five-year grape boycotts from 1965 to 1970 proved much more successful than past campaigns because the union took the fight away from the fields to local consumers. By increasing the scope of the conflict and including sympathetic outsiders, such as political leaders, students, religious institutions, other labor unions, and concerned citizens outside of the area, the UFW was able to win the grape boycott and sign a contract with the grape farmers in 1970. The grape boycotts were followed by lettuce and vegetable boycotts that also led to landmark contracts.

Chavez was the president and charismatic leader of the UFW from its founding until his death in 1993. The UFW had a National Executive Board, which was elected by representatives selected by members, and Chavez was director of the executive board (Ganz 2009). While the board was elected by union members, it is clear that Chavez's vision for the union was primary, and in practice he had veto power over all major decisions. As one participant, who has long been engaged in nonprofit work as well as volunteering for the farm workers, told me:

> He was very conscious of involving people in decision making and he tried to build consensus. He took the time, had the meetings, and people talked through the issues and said their points of view. That is how consensus was built and that is how policy was built. And that is real. On the other hand, Cesar had the final say. I don't know how else to put it.

Chavez also assigned individuals to the top jobs within the union based on their past work, education, and the needs of the union; there was no choice as to the work one did. Kevin, who now works as a union organizer with another large union, told me that in the UFW, "if a big campaign came along, everyone was swept up into that. Whether you were an accountant or an attorney, the needs of the movement came first. And your assignment, whatever that might have been, came second." Consequently, the needs of the union took priority over individual choices of jobs to perform.

In 1971, the headquarters of the UFW was moved from Delano to an old tuberculosis sanatorium in Keene, California. The new headquarters was called "La Paz" (the peace). By this time the UFW comprised 70,000 members including a smaller group of volunteers who lived at La Paz. These volunteers worked on union organizing, boycotts, running campaigns, and other activities; they were paid $5 a week and given room and board while living at La Paz. This core cadre worked for subsistence and supported the union's work with their own labor, supplemented by additional work from short-term volunteers (Ganz 2009).

La Paz provided an intense sense of community. Cynthia describes living at La Paz in the early 1970s: "I think that in this period La Paz provided a community structure and a support system that allowed volunteers to stay longer and burn out less frequently." There were many communal activities, such as eating together in a large cafeteria and sleeping in communal living arrangements. Individuals who lived at La Paz worked long hours six or seven days a week on union business, moving from one campaign to the next without breaks.

The UFW volunteers were and are diverse in a number of respects. While many people think of the UFW as entirely Latino, it is also composed of many whites, Filipinos, and people of other ethnicities. In addition, a wide variety of ages and occupations are represented in the union, from farm workers to college students to lawyers. There were five main groups of UFW volunteers at La Paz when my interviewees lived there in 1971. First, there were Latinos and Filipinos who had worked in the fields themselves or who came from farm worker families. Second, many religious groups and individuals came to La Paz. The National Farm Worker Ministries, in particular, were an important resource for the group; these ministries are interfaith organizations that were founded to support the work of the farm worker union and farm workers generally. In addition, many Catholic, Protestant, and other religious women and men came to La Paz to help in the cause. Third, young people from colleges and universities and those who had dropped out of school were also an important source of volunteer support for the UFW, especially on the picket lines and in support of the boycotts. Fourth, many young attorneys came to La Paz to work for the union in their endless legal battles. Finally, organized labor, including the AFL-CIO and smaller unions, sent individuals to aid in campaigns.

In summary, the UFW is a hierarchically organized group, with a clear leadership and assigned tasks for members. There is a National Executive Board, once led by Chavez; convention delegates; negotiating committees; crew stewards; and elected ranch committees (Ganz 2009). It involves intensive and frequent interaction among the members who live and work at La Paz, the union headquarters. Its scope is narrow and single-issue based. While the members of the group show high levels of commitment to the issue of organizing farm labor and fighting for their rights, the organization and its leadership do not explicitly tie this issue to other leftist issues, such as women's rights or antiwar mobilization. I interviewed 15 activists who lived at La Paz in 1971 (see the Appendix for sampling information and Table 5 for a demographic profile of the group members).

Homeowners Association (Low Hierarchy, Single-issue)

The term "NIMBY" (Not In My Back Yard) encompasses the protectionist attitudes of, and exclusionary and oppositional tactics adopted by, community groups facing an unwelcome development in their neighborhood (Wolch and Dear 1993). Halfway houses, group homes, shelters, and soup kitchens have been common objects of NIMBY mobilization (Snow and Anderson 1993). These groups may be progressive or conservative and are an important and widespread form of organizing occurring in industrialized nations today.

The group examined in this analysis is a homeowners association in Santa Monica, California. The mid- to late 1970s saw many changes in Santa Monica: a steep decline in new construction of multifamily housing units, a vacancy rate below 5 percent, rents increasing faster than the consumer price index, and "an extraordinary increase in building turnover and speculation"—tenfold between 1972 and 1977 (Heskin 1983, 40). A comparative study of local conditions found that between 1970 and 1978, landlords in Santa Monica were increasing their rents more than twice as fast as landlords elsewhere in Southern California. These conditions led to the rise of a renters' rights group called Santa Monicans for Renters Rights (Čapek and Gilderbloom 1992).

The Homeowners Association (HA)[13] was formed in 1981 in reaction to the perceived success of this renters' rights group, which was calling for a sharp increase in low-income housing and a remodeling tax on homes. The renters' rights group represented a large majority of citizens who rented in the city (80%).[14] Some homeowners in the area, feeling underrepresented and unorganized, called a public meeting in 1981. Any interested citizens, preferably homeowners, were welcome to attend this meeting to discuss a counter-campaign. This meeting established a board of directors, a monthly newsletter, and a plan of action to counter the success of the renters' rights group and protect the homeowners' interests in the city.

When discussing why they originally formed the group, one of its founding members, Amy, described how "the issues scared us. The remodeling thing, they were talking about low-income housing everywhere in the city. It was like righting a wrong. I felt like people were trying to take over my city for reasons that were not good for the city and I still think that." The group's main concern was protecting the property values of its members. They feared that home values would be reduced by low-income housing in the area, taxes levied on homeowners, increased traffic in residential areas, and what was perceived as a burgeoning homeless population in the city. They also supported candidates with similar ideologies for local elected office. From 1981 through 1989, the HA distributed monthly newsletters, met monthly, and organized campaigns.

In 1989, the HA commissioned a citywide poll asking homeowners what they felt was the most pressing problem facing the city, and an overwhelming majority of homeowners responded that the homeless population was their primary concern. In response to the widespread interest in this issue, in 1990 the HA became the City Saving Team (CST).[15] The CST limited its mandate to restricting the number of homeless in the city. This new group was composed of the same core individuals as the HA but also included nonhomeowners who were concerned with ridding the city of the homeless. This group continued from 1990 to 1994.

In 1994, some members of the group put forward a citywide initiative called the Public Safety Initiative. A new group, the Citizens for the Public Safety Initiative (CPSI),[16] was formed out of the CST. The initiative called for limiting the use of parks by the homeless, particularly restricting camping in the parks, and called for a $25 fine for this activity. In addition, it mandated a ban on "aggressive" panhandling. The initiative passed in 1994, after which the group dwindled in size and influence. While this group has changed names throughout its history, adapting to the perceived growth of the homeless population and the growing concern about this issue in the city, for simplicity and in reflection of the continuity in its core membership and mission I refer to this group as the Homeowners Association (HA) throughout this discussion.

In general, the HA is concerned that policies sympathetic to the homeless in Santa Monica are resulting in the city becoming a magnet for homeless individuals from around the country. In an article in the Santa Monica *Outlook* from June 22, 1990, Jean Sedillos states:

> Our city's present homeless policy endangers everyone who lives here by attracting transients from all over the country, especially young men who know they can get three free meals a day and camp out in any park, no questions asked.

She says that the homeless "could be supporting themselves, but prefer to travel here, commit crimes and exploit our social services."

The HA's concerns with regard to the homeless population are threefold. First, they are concerned with the impact of the homeless on housing values. Second, they see the homeless population as a threat to personal safety, maintaining that it increases the crime rate. Finally, the HA claims that the presence of the homeless has a negative impact on business and tourism. In this regard, an advertisement run by the HA in a local newspaper asks, "Would you like to take your children to the park? Not be threatened (or worse) on our streets? Go to the beach without fear?"

The HA is a grassroots organization. While it has a board of directors, these individuals are simply the attendees of the first meeting in 1981. Anyone who attended this meeting and who wanted to be involved was invited to be a board member.[17] Amy, a founding member of the group, explained that this board was created specifically to add legitimacy to the group and to ensure that at least a small core of individuals would commit time and energy to the cause. Diana told me that "the leadership in these kinds of groups is always by default. Anyone can be a leader, because no one wants to do it." All positions were voluntary and unpaid. In addition, individuals could contribute as much or as little time as they liked in any position or task they thought was important. As a result, the group made relatively few demands on its members. HA participants worked on a variety of activities: the group published a monthly newsletter and a group of volunteers and board members wrote, edited, and distributed this publication to the homeowners in the city. In addition, some members organized monthly meetings, went to city council events, and organized campaigns for candidates running for city council who were responsive to their concerns.

All of the individuals who became involved in the HA lived in Santa Monica at the time of initial involvement and throughout their engagement. Because of the high cost of living in the area, they were generally of high socioeconomic status. An interesting difference between this group and the others presented in this book is that individuals in this group tended to initially get involved for instrumental reasons: they were concerned about their property values, safety in their parks, or traffic on their streets. In fact, Diana, a 70-year-old manager, expressed this instrumental commitment when she told me: "I won't go to meetings unless it affects my particular three blocks." In addition, with only three exceptions, none of the individuals in the HA with whom I spoke had ever been involved in other types of social protest, and some did not engage in contentious tactics (such as protesting, demonstrating, or marching) even while participating in this group. Thus the participants in this group were of a somewhat different character from and viewed their participation in less contentious terms than did the individuals in the other three groups.

In summary, the HA is a grassroots and nonhierarchical organization. It does not involve an explicit leadership or hierarchical power relationships among its members. The interaction in the group is not frequent or intimate in nature, and the group's scope is narrow and single-issue based. While there is agreement on reducing the number of homeless in the city, the group does not work on other linked issues. I interviewed 15 participants from the original meeting in 1981 (see the Appendix for sampling procedures and Table 5 for demographic information).

Respondents

As shown in Table 5, the Catholic Workers I interviewed range in age from 53 to 81 (and were, on average, 25.87 years old when they initially participated in 1970). I spoke with nine men and six women. A large majority of the respondents have at least a bachelor's degree (86%) and the same number work in a professional[18] occupation. Nine respondents identify as Catholic, although they practice to varying degrees; one identifies as mainline Protestant; and five designate themselves as having no religious affiliation.

The Concerned Women for America interviewed are, of course, all women. Their education varies, with all having a high school diploma and 53 percent having a bachelor's degree or more. All the women I interviewed are or had been married and have children. They also all identify as Protestant, with 73 percent identifying as evangelical or "born again" Christians. They were, interestingly, of similar ages as the CWs at the time of the interview, which indicates that they were, on average, 10 years older (37) than the CWs when they initially got involved in their group (as I interviewed CWAs active in 1981 and CWs active in 1970).

The United Farm Workers interviewed are 40 percent female. A large majority have a bachelor's or more advanced degree (80%), and 93 percent work in professional occupations. Most have been married (73%) and have children (87%). The majority of the sample are Catholic (80%) but attend religious services less than twice a month (73%). When they participated in the 1970s, the mean age of the sample was 25, and they were, on average, 61 years old at the time of the interview.

The Homeowners Association members are predominantly female (73%) and also have high levels of education, with 80 percent having a bachelor's or more advanced degree. While two-thirds of this group work in professional occupations, 27 percent are homemakers. The majority of the group (80%) have been married, but only 60 percent have children. The religion of the group members is highly varied, with one-third identifying as nonreligious; 40 percent of this sample never attend religious services. The mean age at the time of interview was 64, and thus the respondents were 38 years old at the time of the founding of the group in 1981.

In order to assess the representativeness of my sample, I compare it with the national sample of individuals discussed in Chapters 2 and 3 who have ever engaged in a social movement organization. Because the panel sample follows individuals from 1965, when they were high school seniors, to 1997, they are approximately the same age as my qualitative sample. The 1960 census sample mirrors my sample in terms of marital status and childbearing. My sample slightly overrepresents Catholics (as one of my groups was Catholic) but shows similar levels of religiosity. My sample is also slightly more educated. For sociodemographic information about my respondents, together with a comparison of my sample with the nationally representative sample, see Table 5.

As shown in Table 6, most of the CWs continued to participate in social movements over time. Only three (20%) disengaged, while one (7%) persisted in the same group, seven (47%) transferred their participation to another group, and four (27%) experienced an abeyance trajectory of participation over time. The story is somewhat different for the CWAs, who show an interesting dichotomy in their participation trajectories. Sixty-seven percent disengaged and 27 percent persisted, with only one individual in a middle trajectory (transferring to another group). Of the UFW sample, 33 percent (5) persisted, while 27 percent transferred and 20 percent followed an abeyance trajectory. An additional 20 percent of the UFW volunteers I interviewed disengaged from participation completely. Finally, 73 percent of the HA sample disengaged from this group and participation as a whole, 20 percent (3) transferred to another group, and 7 percent (1) engaged in abeyance. None of the participants in the HA persisted in participation over time.

The average length of participation in the group was longest for the UFW (18.33 years), followed by the CW (12.13 years), the HA (7.53 years), and CWA (6.85 years). In general, the pattern of participation of my sample over time is very similar to that of the national population, although the national sample is marginally more likely to disengage. This is partly due to my selection of two groups that required relatively high levels of commitment initially, the Catholic Workers and the United Farm Workers. For information about the participation of my sample and the national sample over time, see Table 6.

Discussion and Conclusion

Past work on participation in social movements beyond initial engagement has relied on either large national surveys or individual case studies. Both of these methods have illuminated certain predictors of sustained engagement over time, while obfuscating others. On the one hand, large national

Table 6 Participation over time by group

	Catholic Workers	Concerned Women for America	United Farm Workers	Homeowners Association	Total (four groups)	Jennings Panel sample[a]
Persist	7%	27%	33%	0%	17%	20%
	(1)	(4)	(5)	(0)	(10)	
Transfer	47%	7%	27%	20%	25%	
	(7)	(1)	(4)	(3)	(15)	
Abeyance	27%	0%	20%	7%	13%	38%
	(4)	(0)	(3)	(1)	(8)	
Disengage	20%	67%	20%	73%	45%	42%
	(3)	(10)	(3)	(11)	(27)	
Years of engagement in focal group						
Mean	12.13	6.85	18.33	7.53	11.21	
Range	(2–36)	(0.25–23)	(5–41)	(3–20)	(0.25–41)	

[a]Data derived from Jennings and Stoker (2004). For more information, see the Appendix.

surveys can examine ideology, resources, biographical availability, and socio-demographic predictors of engagement but fail to explain the role of the context in which participation occurs. On the other hand, individual case studies can provide a more in-depth understanding of some of these factors but fail to assess the effect of organizational structure on participation, as only one organizational context is examined at a time.

The organizational and relational context of participation, including the level of hierarchy, issue scope, and intensity of social interaction, are important parts of my overall model of movement participation as outlined in Chapter 1. These contextual factors affect an individual's experience of participation and whether she will remain in a social movement over time. This is because these factors shape the identities individuals create and the social ties they form within social movements. In turn, these identities and ties make it more or less likely that individuals will persist in their movement organizations over time.

The relationships between these contextual factors and identity and social ties are the subject of the following two chapters. Chapter 5 examines the role of social ties and member interaction in predicting participation over time. Chapter 6 assesses the role of identity in accounting for trajectories of participation in the four groups studied. Both of these chapters pay particular attention to the effect of organizational and relational structure and show how this structure is related to the strength and direction of these relationships.

5 The Ties That Bind?

The Effect of Social Ties and Interaction

SOCIAL TIES ARE A KEY MEANS by which individuals become involved in social movements and contentious politics. David's recruitment to the United Farm Workers illustrates the significance of these ties. In 1969, while he was attending college in California, David met one of Cesar Chavez's eight children. After getting to know one another in their American history class, they started going to the weekend pickets that were part of the grape boycott of 1969. Over time, David met more people in the farm worker movement, and in 1971, after he graduated from college, David was introduced to Cesar Chavez himself. Chavez invited David to move to La Paz and work for the union as a media liaison. David accepted this offer and worked closely with Chavez for 10 years. During his time at La Paz, he became very close friends with many of the other volunteers with whom he worked and lived communally. One of these people, Anna, became his wife in 1974. They had three children. By 1981, however, no longer able to live on the $10 a week the union paid (an increase from the $5 a week he had been paid when he moved to La Paz 10 years earlier), David moved back to Los Angeles with his wife and children. When I spoke with him in 2005, David was still organizing media campaigns for the UFW and other unions, mostly on a volunteer basis. He still has many close friends in the group and remains married to Anna, who is also still an active member of the UFW.

Social ties were also an important component of Ellen's mobilization to contentious politics. In 1980, Ellen heard a speech given by Beverly LaHaye. After the speech, LaHaye asked Ellen if she would be willing to found a prayer action chapter of Concerned Women for America in her city. Ellen was able to recruit four other women who had also attended the speech to the first meeting of the prayer group. This group of women then continued to meet about once a month in the basement of a local Protestant church. They did not know one another before joining this group and did not have a chance to become friends as the meetings were short and infrequent. It was also difficult for Ellen to spend much time participating in CWA as she had five children and worked full-time as a teacher. After six months, Ellen stopped attending the meetings. The local chapter dissipated one month later. Ellen never again participated in other social movement groups or protest activities.

As the stories of David and Ellen illustrate, social ties are an important part of how individuals are recruited to social movements, and these ties can facilitate continued participation over time. For David, a friend recruited him to the group; he formed close ties within the group; and he has remained connected to other participants over the course of his life. These ties were an important part of how David was able to sustain his participation over time. In contrast, Ellen did not know others in the group when she joined, she did not make close friends in the group, and as a result she lost contact with others in the group when she left. For Ellen, the lack of social bonds within the group, together with competing work and family demands, partly explains her short-term participation and permanent disengagement from the organization.

The model of movement participation outlined in Chapter 1 (Figure 1) emphasizes the role of social ties in social movements and contentious political participation. In this model, I highlight how the structure and character of social movement organizations shape the number, type, and intensity of ties that develop in the course of participation. The comparative analysis of four different social movement organizations allows for an examination of how key elements of an organization's structure and character shape these ties and, in turn, an individual's participation over time. In the next section, I outline past research on the role of social ties in contentious political participation. I examine how social ties work as a motivation for recruitment, build solidarity within groups, and help individuals sustain their engagement over the course of their lives.

The Role of Social Ties

As social movement activities are usually embedded in dense relational settings (Diani 2004), the probability that an individual will join an organization depends upon the number and strength of social ties that connect group members to each other and to nonmembers (McPherson et al. 1992). As a result, integration into social networks can draw individuals into social movements (McAdam 1986), and because of this, individuals who are well integrated into a community are more likely to engage in these organizations (Useem 1998).

Many empirical studies have demonstrated the importance of social ties for social movement mobilization. For example, the Southern sit-in movement of the 1960s developed out of preexisting social networks formed inside churches, colleges, and protest organizations (Morris 1981). The same is true of feminist mobilization—women who were connected through networks were more likely to mobilize and participate in the movement (Freeman 1975). These personal networks of friends provide individual incentives to participate in social movements (Opp and Gern 1993). They also create a gateway for participation and lower the costs of engagement for individuals. In light of the foregoing, it is not surprising that past research repeatedly finds that the presence of a social tie to someone already engaged in a movement is one of the strongest predictors of individual participation (see, e.g., Gould 1990; Marwell et al. 1988; McAdam and Paulsen 1993; Nepstad and Smith 1999; Passy and Giugni 2001; Snow et al. 1980).

Other scholars have examined how various types of ties may impact recruitment. Ties can vary in terms of their strength and content; strong ties with other activists have a more powerful effect on recruitment than weak ties (Brady et al. 1999; Gould 2004; McAdam 1986; McAdam and Paulsen 1993). Generally, people are more likely to participate in political activities when asked by a close friend than when asked by a stranger or an acquaintance (Brady et al. 1999; Klandermans 1984). This is because, when one is recruited by a close friend, the rewards of participation and the cost of nonparticipation are higher (Kitts 2000; McAdam 1986).

In addition to serving as predictors of social movement participation, social ties may also be created and strengthened in the course of participation once individuals are involved in groups. Social ties are, therefore, both precipitants of recruitment and outcomes of the process of engagement. The ties created within social movements can foster the growth of group solidarity and strengthen commitment to the group and its cause (Cress et al. 1997; Kanter 1968). For example, Hirsch's (1990) study of a university divestment blockade highlights the importance of social ties formed within movements and shows how these ties keep people involved. This work demonstrates that strong ties help participants deal with the emotional impact of hard times during campaigns. In addition, Snow and Phillips's (1980) study of the Nichiren Shoshu Buddhist movement in the United States shows that intensive interaction and affective bonds created in the context of movement participation are critical in member conversion, an important factor leading to continued engagement over time.

One way social ties are created and reinforced is through shared participation in cultural practices and group rituals. Rituals are symbolic embodiments of the beliefs and feelings of a group. They bring like-minded individuals together on a regular basis and rejuvenate the emotional bonds and relational ties that strengthen affective commitment and keep members integrated into groups. Collective rituals remind participants of their moral commitment to the group, stir up strong emotions, and reinforce group solidarity (Jasper 1998).

Informal ritual interaction is critical for creating strong ties among members. Blumer (1969) and others have hypothesized that engagement in informal fellowship and ceremonial behavior is important to the esprit de corps and morale of a group (see also Fine and Stoecker 1985; Neitz 1987). Informal fellowship refers to occasions in which members have the opportunity to come to know one another personally and to develop a common sympathy and sense of intimacy. This may be as simple as informal conversations between members but could also include singing, dancing, and other communal activities. Previous studies have demonstrated the importance of these types of ritual events, such as prayer meetings, rallies, consciousness-raising groups, and late-night discussion sessions (Fantasia 1988; Hirsch 1990; Nepstad 2004; Taylor and Whittier 1995; for a discussion see Cohn et al. 2003).

In addition to the interaction among group members, some organizations encourage and enable interaction between participants and the constituency they aim to help, which can create strong friendships. Of course, not all interaction between participants and constituents fosters social ties. Some work on what is labeled "plug-in style" volunteering finds that many individuals interact with a constituency they aim to help in a very impersonal way, which fails to create strong ties and friendships. Lichterman's study of a volunteer organization he calls "Fun Evenings" illustrates the often superficial ways in which volunteers and constituents, in this case at-risk teenagers, may interact. He finds that volunteers were encouraged to take a perspective of "wary watchfulness and cordial distance" (2005, 544). Such types of interaction are unlikely to foster personal friendships.

Social ties formed with other participants through the course of engagement can last long after individuals leave a social movement organization. Even when individuals leave a specific SMO, they often remain friends with people they met during their participation (McAdam 1988). In this chapter, I assess the extent to which these ties contribute to an individual's likelihood of persisting in their participation or reengaging in contentious politics later in life if they leave their group.

The Role of Organizations

As discussed above, social ties are an important part of how individuals are recruited to organizations. Once individuals are members of an organization, these ties can foster feelings of solidarity and attachment to the group and other members. Not all groups, however, are structured in a way that facilitates the growth of social ties, and groups differ in the extent to which they are able to create and sustain these ties over time. In particular, elements of group context, such as the degree of hierarchy within the group and the level of interaction among members, affect the number, type, and duration of the social ties individuals create in the course of participation. This chapter highlights the importance of these elements of organizational structure for the creation of social ties and, consequently, the continuity of individual participation over time.

Groups differ in terms of their degree of hierarchy and are arrayed on a continuum from egalitarian to hierarchical. Hierarchical organizations are both more formalized and centralized than egalitarian groups. Formalization refers to the degree to which an SMO has an explicit written scheme of organization and division of labor. Centralization is the degree to which an SMO's activities are directed by a well-identified leadership as opposed to originating from multiple, relatively independent SMO subgroupings. While these two characteristics can vary independently, they tend to be strongly correlated. An SMO that is highly formalized is also likely to be highly centralized.

The degree of organizational hierarchy is significant in two ways. First, it affects the ability of group members to create social ties with other members. In egalitarian groups, opportunities for social interaction often abound, allowing for the creation of strong ties among participants. Hierarchical groups provide fewer opportunities of this nature and hence are less likely to create mutual ties. Hierarchical groups, however, may be able to overcome this limitation by developing a federated structure involving local chapters. Past work on large national SMOs suggests that the creation of local chapters that meet regularly can strengthen social ties among group members even within large hierarchical groups (Lofland and Jamison 1984; McCarthy and Zald 1977). While these claims are logical, there have been few empirical studies that examine the effect of local chapters and federated structures on member participation over time; the analysis provided here will shed light on this issue.

Second, the degree of hierarchy within the group affects the recruitment methods used in the organization. In hierarchical organizations, leaders are more likely to actively recruit new members. Hierarchical groups are also more likely to have individuals whose sole task within the organization is recruitment, who may act as the face of the organization when attracting new members. In more egalitarian groups, recruitment is conducted by rank-and-file members, as there are no formal leaders and it is less likely that there will be specialization that will result in particular individuals being charged with the sole task of recruitment. Instead, recruitment is often simply one of many tasks that a variety of individual members perform. In this analysis, I examine the effect of these different modes of recruitment in order to assess the extent to which hierarchical and egalitarian groups differ in their recruitment strategies and the ways in which this affects the continuity of individual engagement over time.

Drawing on the interview data discussed in Chapter 4, I assess how the organizational and relational structure, in particular the degree of hierarchy and intensity of interaction within the group, are related to the ability of groups to create and sustain social ties. Then I examine the effect of these ties on an individual's trajectory of participation over time.

Preengagement Ties in Four Contexts

Most participants in the four social movement organizations in this analysis were recruited through social ties. In fact, 95 percent (57 of 60) of the people I interviewed knew others active in the groups prior to joining.[1] Clearly, consistent with what a large body of literature already asserts, social ties are an important medium for mobilizing individuals to join SMOs. There are a variety of individuals, however, occupying different social locations within the organization who are involved in new member recruitment. Past work has assessed the importance of different types of social ties, particularly examining the strength and content of the ties and focusing on how these different types of ties impact the success of the mobilization effort. In this analysis, I argue that the social location of the recruiter is also significant because it im-

Table 7 Prerecruitment ties to rank-and-file members by trajectory of participation

		Trajectory			
Group	Knew rank-and-file member	Disengage (%) (N = 27)	Abeyance (%) (N = 8)	Transfer (%) (N = 15)	Persist (%) (N = 10)
Catholic	Yes (N = 15)	20	27	47	7
Workers	No (N = 0)	—	—	—	—
Concerned	Yes (N = 2)	—	—	50	50
Women for	No (N = 13)	77	—	—	23
America					
United Farm	Yes (N = 7)	—	43	14	43
Workers	No (N = 8)	38	—	38	25
Homeowners	Yes (N = 9)	56	11	33	—
Association	No (N = 6)	100	—	—	—
Total	Yes (N = 33)	24	24	36	15
	No (N = 27)	70	—	11	19

NOTE: Fisher's exact test is significant at p-value < 0.001.

pacts the trajectory of participation of the recruited. So, not only does the nature of the tie impact whether or not an individual joins but it also affects the length and continuity of the individual's participation over time. Thus, features of the recruitment process itself are significant for their long-term effects on participation once an individual is involved.

In short, individuals may know rank-and-file members, those who are not in leadership positions and with whom they have lateral social ties, or they may know people in leadership positions, with whom they have hierarchical social ties. Table 7 shows that individuals who personally knew rank-and-file members before their initial involvement are more likely to persist and less likely to disengage than those who did not have these lateral personal relationships.[2]

While individuals who were recruited by leaders are less likely to remain engaged over time than those who were recruited by rank-and-file members, interaction with leaders once involved in the group is a key factor in mitigating the negative effect of being recruited by a leader. Table 8 demonstrates that in groups with high levels of interaction, in which members have contact with the leaders who recruited them, individuals are much less likely to disengage over time than in groups with little interaction between the new members and the leaders who recruited them.[3] Thus, it is both the character of the recruiter and the extent of interaction with the recruiter once involved that predicts an individual's trajectory of participation.

The source of mobilization, whether leaders or rank-and-file members, is related to the structure of the organization as a whole. In more egalitarian groups (such as the Catholic Workers and the Homeowners Association), there are fewer or no specialized leadership positions.[4] As a result, if individuals are personally recruited to participate, they are, by definition, recruited by rank-and-file members. In contrast, groups that are more hierarchical tend to have specialized leaders, and in these groups individuals are often recruited through their hierarchical social ties with these leaders. In hierarchical organizations (such as CWA and the UFW), those recruited by leaders are less likely to persist and more likely to disengage over time than are individuals who are recruited by rank-and-file members. These relationships will be illustrated in more detail by examining each of the four group contexts.

In the less hierarchical Catholic Workers and Homeowners Association, rank-and-file members provided the impetus for recruitment. All of the individuals who joined the CW knew people who lived in the communal houses before they joined the group. This was because the group was not very vis-

Table 8 Effect of recruiter type on trajectory of participation for hierarchical groups

		Trajectory			
Group	Recruiter	Disengage (%) (N = 13)	Abeyance (%) (N = 3)	Transfer (%) (N = 5)	Persist (%) (N = 9)
High Interaction					
United Farm Workers	Leader (N = 8)	25	13	38	25
	Rank and file (N = 7)	14	28	14	43
Low Interaction					
Concerned Women for America	Leader (N = 13)	77	—	—	23
	Rank and file (N = 2)	—	—	50	50
TOTAL	Leader (N = 21)	57	5	14	24
	Rank and file (N = 9)	11	22	22	44

NOTES: All individuals in the CW and HA were recruited by rank-and-file members as there were no official leaders in these groups.

Fisher's exact test is significant at p-value < 0.01.

ible in the mainstream media, so that individuals who joined had to know others through personal networks. Harriet, for example, made friendships with CW community members through her volunteer work at a crisis center for people at risk of homelessness. Neal, who later worked at a nonprofit agency, met CW members through Catholic antiwar groups. Arnold, a librarian, explained how many individuals in the CW came from a group called the Catholic Peace Movement, active in the 1960s, in which they were primarily learning about current conditions in Vietnam. These ties existed before recruitment to the CW community and tended to be personal ties with rank-and-file members of the group.

The importance of recruitment by rank-and-file members is most pronounced in groups where there is intensive interaction among members in the course of participation. Interaction postrecruitment is much higher in communal groups such as the CW, because individuals tend to interact more intensely with their recruiters in the process of participation. In particular, such groups engage in volunteer activities that are, by nature, group efforts. The CWs make meals for the homeless, run a coffeehouse for troubled teens, and operate a shelter for abused women. These are all ventures that require group effort. Members spend large amounts of time together, strengthening their affective bonds while working on these activities, which is partly the result of the more communal and unstructured nature of the group.

Social ties with rank-and-file members were also an important route to participation in the Homeowners Association. In the HA, 60 percent (9 of 15) of the interviewees had ties to rank-and-file members of the group before joining. In every case, however, these ties were not close personal friends but simply acquaintances from the neighborhood or from other local groups. For instance, Anna became involved because her neighbor told her about the initial meeting; Ruth met a participant through her local PTA; and Polly answered the door to a neighbor she had not previously met who recruited her to a meeting. In effect, individuals tended to be recruited through weak ties with other rank-and-file members. Although these individuals did interact with their recruiters once involved in the group, the relationships remained at a casual level.

In this group, because there was little intensive interaction after initial recruitment, weak ties were not strengthened in the course of participation. Instead of working on larger communal projects, like the CWs, HA members worked on more solitary voluntary activities, such as writing group publications, distributing the newsletter, or talking to the media. Individuals engaged in these activities alone, in isolation from other volunteers. For example, Diana acted as the treasurer for the group and was in charge of filing the necessary forms to maintain the group's tax-exempt status. She was sent receipts and other documents in the mail by the board members once every two or three months and then completed the paperwork on her own. She did not have to see or talk with other group members in order to perform this task. These kinds of activities, which were partly the result of the less communal nature of the group, made the creation or strengthening of social ties between group members less likely.

In contrast, in a hierarchical group such as CWA, leaders are a critical part of the recruitment process. In fact, 87 percent (13 of 15) of new recruits in the group were personally mobilized to participate by a leader, while only 13 percent (2 of 15) of the participants were recruited by other rank-and-file members. It is clear that the general mode of recruitment was through ties with national or state leaders, as in the case of Joanne, who was asked to lead her state chapter by the national leader, Beverly LaHaye. While these ties were highly effective at initially mobilizing individuals, the lack of interaction with leaders after initial recruitment made the ties difficult to sustain.

Once a woman was involved in CWA, she subsequently had very little interaction with the leader who recruited her. The lack of interaction with leaders after initial engagement meant that these relationships were not solidified over time. Emily's mobilization illustrates this: She became involved in CWA when a state leader called her mother's house, where she was staying while her mother was out of town. The leader was calling to recruit her mother, who had donated money to the organization in the past, to help organize a conference in her area. As her mother was not available, Emily offered to help organize the event. She called approximately 150 women to inform them of the event and organized the food for the meeting. Although one other woman in the area was also involved in the organizing effort, Emily never personally met her and only talked with her on the phone on three occasions. After the conference, Emily was never again contacted by the state leader who had initially recruited her or by any other CWA members. While she continued to receive the newsletters and pay membership dues for the next six months, she was never an active participant in the group again. CWA is structured with isolated federated units throughout the country that have little ongoing contact with the national or state leadership. Because of this, individuals who were recruited by this national or state leadership were not in regular contact with their recruiters and were unable to create and maintain personal relationships with them over time.

While some women in CWA did have ties to rank-and-file members, such as family members who were in the group, they were never proximate. For example, Sally heard about the group through her mother-in-law, who was in a CWA chapter in another state. Members of the families of the women with whom I talked always participated in another city or state, and so, once an individual was involved in her local group, she did not have regular contact with another family member who was also involved. For this reason, even the ties with other rank-and-file recruiters were not strengthened through group participation.

In the United Farm Workers, another hierarchical group, individuals also tended to be recruited either by leaders, such as Cesar Chavez himself, or by individuals closely tied to leaders, such as Chavez's children or other relatives. In fact, over half of the respondents (8 of 15) specifically cited a personal relationship either with Chavez or with his immediate family as a critical factor in their decision to participate. Anthony, who now works as a union organizer, met Chavez when working with his parents, who were involved in the union. Others, such as Bert, a priest who went to La Paz in 1971, met Chavez through work in the Catholic Church.

As with CWA, many UFW members were initially recruited through ties with leaders. What differentiates the UFW from CWA, however, is that once individuals became involved in the UFW, there was extensive interaction between them and the leaders who recruited them, including Chavez himself. Because Chavez lived at La Paz, when individuals moved to the headquarters they had regular contact with him and his family, albeit often from afar. This contact solidified relationships and strengthened the ties individuals had with Chavez and other leaders over time.

For example, David came to work at La Paz after being personally recruited by Cesar Chavez, whom he had met through Chavez's son, a close college friend. Once at La Paz, David had a lot of professional and personal contact with Chavez and other leaders. Professionally, he interacted often with Chavez as he worked on media strategy and speech writing for the union. Personally, he often saw Chavez at social events at La Paz because he and other leaders regularly participated in activities such as tending the communal gardens on weekends and attending weddings and other celebrations.

At these events, David and other participants were able to interact with, or at least see and observe, Chavez. These events, made possible by the non-hierarchical communal structure of La Paz, facilitated the creation and maintenance of social ties with some of the leaders involved in recruitment.

Individuals are pulled into social movement activity by a variety of differently situated people. These different ties affect individuals' future trajectories of participation. Delineating how the structure of an organization impacts the way in which individual members interact with their recruiter over time illustrates how the elements of organizational context can affect individual experiences within groups. The amount and intensity of interaction between the recruiter and the recruited, once involved, is a powerful predictor of an individual's trajectory of participation over the life course.

Interaction and Ties within Groups

While social ties lay the foundation for initial participation, they can also be created or strengthened through the process of engagement. Social ties are more likely to emerge and be strengthened when there is a sense of community among members and participants engage in joint ritual behavior. Not all groups, however, are equally capable of, or interested in, doing these things. In general, I argue that communal groups, which involve high levels of interaction and joint participation in ritual behaviors, are more successful at creating a sense of community and strong ties between members. In turn, individuals with stronger ties and who are more integrated into a community of participants tend to remain active for longer periods of time. Groups that are less communal and that involve less joint ritual activity are less successful at creating social ties, which makes participation more difficult to sustain over time.

The Catholic Worker group in my sample was founded on a strong sense of community and ties to the neighborhood in which it was situated. In fact, many group members reported being initially attracted to the group because of its communal atmosphere. Chris, who now works as a social worker, told me that "it was a diverse group of people, but I think that people just shared a desire to make changes and live in a community. That was probably the biggest characteristic that brought people together in the neighborhood." Many individuals, who had been working on similar causes before joining the group, explained that they joined the CW group because they were "looking for more of a support group" rather than simply volunteering for an organization.

In this group, social ties provided strong support for the ongoing participation of members. These ties were built and solidified through the informal socializing that occurred in the communal houses. Janet, a longtime ESL teacher in her community, describes how the CWs "did a lot of socializing. We smoked cigarettes endlessly and drank coffee endlessly and sat up all night talking about things." The fact that joint volunteer activity and paid employment coincided further strengthened the ties among participants. Phil, a 55-year-old social worker, noted:

> What I did as part of my job and what I did as part of the community almost weren't separate. And the people I worked with during the day and the evening and weekends were the same people. It was the same group of people who would be working on whatever community issues there were.

These social ties created support for the members' continued participation. As Phil explained, "Staying involved and having energy and enthusiasm is really dependent on primary relationships with people. I was really close to the [Catholic Workers] and I really liked and admired them. I got a lot of positive feedback from them." In essence, while working on social justice was a primary reason to be in the group in the first place, members like Phil were also strongly motivated to be part of a community or social network of like-minded people. Through moving into communal housing, the CW members sought both to create community within the group as well as to foster the development of community in the neighborhood as a whole. A priest who had long worked with a variety of social justice groups in the neighborhood explained that "we wanted to form a more intentional community ourselves and we wanted to intentionally create a community fabric in the neighborhood."

The communal nature of the group involved high levels of interaction and shared engagement in ritual activities. As discussed previously, Blumer (1969) and others have hypothesized that ritual activities and ceremonial behavior are important to the esprit de corps and morale of a group. This was certainly the case in the CW community. Initially the group had weekly meetings, but these meetings were soon canceled because the group members saw each other so often through volunteer work and just "hanging out" that the meetings became redundant. Other ritual activities in the group were the annual Solstice Festival[5] and monthly potluck dinners—"big community gatherings" that brought together several hundred people in the community. Both the Solstice Festival and the dinners continue to reunite present and past community members and solidify social ties and bonds within the group. The festival and dinners are particularly important because they support ties with past members even after they are no longer actively engaged with the group.

Participation in the UFW also created strong ties and a sense of community among group members. The residents of La Paz worked together, lived together, socialized together, and became "like a family." Anthony, who now works as a union organizer for another large union and who reengaged in a number of waves of participation with the UFW, says, "We were very close friends. You almost had to be. You lived together; you slept next to each other on the floor and sometimes on the road." The close ties created at La Paz were partially the result of La Paz's physically isolated location. David, a longtime resident of La Paz, aptly states that "you had to socialize with other UFW volunteers. There was no one else." The intensity of the atmosphere at La Paz, with the long working hours and rigorous campaigns, also contributed to solidifying friendships within the organization.

Ritual interaction, in the form of weekly meetings, strengthened the social ties and feeling of community created in the UFW. Group meetings were based on the shared Catholic experience of many of the group members and were inspired by African American Protestant church culture. They included singing, speeches, witnessing, prayer, and other ritualized activities. Holidays, such as Cesar Chavez's birthday, Mexican Independence Day, and weddings, also brought individuals together. Furthermore, community was intentionally created and sustained through activities such as caring for the communal gardens. One man, who had to leave La Paz because his wife became ill but who continued to engage in farm worker–related issues, explained:

> For awhile on Saturdays instead of working in the office, [Cesar] would have everyone go out to work in the garden and have meals served and have lunch brought out and make a big deal about it. He wanted people to do things together. He was trying to found some kind of communal society.

Social ties were particularly important in the UFW because they helped sustain participation over time even when campaigns became intense and difficult. As Charlie explained, "People who came in groups or who got to know others at La Paz tended to last longer and I think that one of the reasons for that was that they had a better support system." Because of this, single people and young people who came to La Paz often remained for shorter periods of time than individuals who came as part of a larger social network. As Charlie puts it, people who came through the National Farm Worker Ministry had "more backup." These ties and the sense of community structure and support they created allowed volunteers to "burn out" less frequently.

Social ties were also important because they made difficulties seem less insurmountable. Again, as Charlie explains, "Seeing the commitment of the other volunteers made you realize what you could do yourself. You see other people who are giving up everything and it makes you feel like you can continue to give up everything yourself for the cause too." This high level of interaction ensured that individuals saw others' hard work and dedication, and over time this dedication came to be seen as worthy of emulating by other members of the group.

There are risks, however, associated with the intense social ties created within communal groups such as the UFW and the CW. When these bonds were broken or friendships ended, it was very difficult for individuals to continue to participate in these groups. For example, many members of the CW and UFW married other participants within the group. This is not surprising, given the amount of time most of the activists spent working within the group and the communal nature of the living arrangements. In the event these relationships ended, however, it became difficult for both former spouses to comfortably remain within these tight-knit communities.

Jeremy is a case in point: he left the CW after 14 years of participation as a result of his divorce. He had been living communally in a home with his wife and two other families. After his divorce, the shared living arrangement became more difficult, and he felt compelled to move out of the communal home and then, not long after, left the group entirely. In groups with less interaction and a less communal environment, Jeremy might have been able to continue participating, but the amount of interaction this would require with his ex-wife in the context of a communal group such as the CW made this impossible. In groups with such intense ties, major biographical changes, such as having children, marrying, or divorcing, can alter one's relationship to the group and one's ability to remain actively involved over time.

In CWA, a less communal group, women came to the group with ties to either the leadership or a nonproximate family member who was also involved. In both of these situations, women were recruited by individuals with whom they would not have much interaction once they were involved in the group. There was, however, a realization at the organizational level that this lack of interaction could pose problems for retaining members over time. The women

I interviewed who were state leaders talked about an organizational policy of attempting to intentionally create social ties in the group "to maintain individuals in the organization." While women like Christine, a state leader who had been a member for 20 years, told me that she "didn't join CWA for social reasons," she quickly acknowledged the importance of social ties with other members. Indeed, she had been encouraged by the national leadership to foster such ties, when they told her that "you recruit through vision, you maintain through relationships." In this way, the national leadership was attempting to foster these sorts of relationships to strengthen members' commitment to the organization.

As a result of this strategy, many of the women in leadership positions in CWA did develop close friendships. Sally, who was also a state leader, became good friends with the other women in her prayer action chapter. She attended her associate leader's wedding and another group member's son's high school graduation. Penny, who was also a state leader, describes her friendships with the women in her prayer action chapter as so close that they were "almost sisters."

Despite these close ties among some of the women in leadership positions, there was very little interaction for the average CWA participant. There was no sense of community in the group and very few close friendships developed. Many rank-and-file members said they "never really [knew] the other women in the group," "did not have much contact with anyone from the group," "didn't go to any meetings," or "did not know one person" in their hometown who was also involved in the group.

This lack of interaction among CWA members was related to the ways in which group members were recruited and the overall structure of the organization. Individuals tended to be recruited by organizational leaders, either at the state or national level. This often occurred when a group leader would individually recruit a woman to start a prayer action chapter at a church event or speech. After the initial recruitment, however, these women were never again contacted by the individual state or national leader who recruited them. While they did receive newsletters from the head office in Washington with information about the group and its activities, there was very little other support for the new prayer action leaders over time. Thus the large federated structure of CWA led to the recruitment of many new leaders to start new chapters, but the large size of the group made it difficult for the national and state leadership to foster the continued participation of women over time.

As a result of the lack of social ties to other members in CWA, a large group of women in this organization who were seeking a feeling of community left the group to participate more actively in their churches, organizations with similar beliefs but that involved more interaction and a feeling of community. Shirley, who was very active in her Evangelical church, describes why she stopped participating in CWA: "I now go to my church every week. I think Beverly [LaHaye] is great, but I prefer to go to my church where I see friends and family." Given their mandate, one would expect CWA to have incorporated prayer into their activities, but surprisingly this was rarely the case. Although Penny was involved in a CWA group that engaged in prayer, a highly ritualized activity that created a sense of community for her and kept her active over time, in fact very few local groups engaged in this kind of ritual activity. This is surprising given the national CWA's explicit focus on prayer as a tactic and the creation of prayer action chapters at the grassroots level. The lack of community in CWA and minimal participation in ritual activity reduced the sense of solidarity in the group. As a result, the women were less likely to remain active in the organization over time. Thus the structural arrangement of the group, particularly the lack of attention paid to fostering social ties and a sense of community or engaging in ritualized activities that required participants to spend time together, significantly affected the participation trajectories of the women in the group.

The Homeowners Association was also less successful at, and perhaps less interested in, creating and fostering a sense of community among members. This group's aim was much narrower than that of the other organizations and individual participants saw their engagement in instrumental terms. Ruth, a lawyer who fell into abeyance after four years in the group, told me that individuals came to this group with weak ties to one another and often saw themselves as "similarly committed residents, not a group of friends." While the group did initially get together for monthly meetings, this did not foster strong ties among members, partly because, as one female member noted, they "did not socialize outside the group." Amy, a stay-at-home mother who transferred from the HA to another group after 16 years, said that while they would work on projects together, they did not "go over and eat dinner together. There had to be a project or something in order for people to get together." The lack of social ties in the group was in part a result of the more instrumental nature of the organization as well as the lack of common issues (besides housing) over which to bond. Because the group members were both

Democrats and Republicans, they often had little else in common politically besides their shared interest in removing the homeless from the area.

I find that groups that encourage informal interaction and the growth of personal relationships between participants and the constituency they aim to help are more likely to foster the development of social ties over time, which, in turn, motivates individuals to remain active. The development of personal ties with a constituency was a regular occurrence in both the Catholic Workers and the United Farm Workers. In both of these groups, face-to-face interaction with individuals they were trying to help was an important motivation for group members to remain with the organization, even in difficult times. For example, Karen, a UFW volunteer who now works as a social worker, stated that "it was really great when you could get people, farm workers, who were working in the fields, some of whom can't read and write, and get them together with people who are educated from all walks of life. We learned so much from the farm workers." James worked with the UFW for 12 years and now works in a job specifically related to educating the public on farm worker issues. He remembers:

> What I loved the most was when we would have farm workers come to Keene, California, and Cesar would be talking with them. And the farm workers would tell stories and share their experiences. We would train them to go on the boycott. I loved the interaction and watching how the farm workers would get this different mindset. Here they are, farm workers, and then all of a sudden they get this empowerment and they are going to go off to the cities and work on a boycott. That was an incredible transformation and it was great.

The Catholic Workers also regularly interacted with individuals they were seeking to help. This occurred at the nightly dinners for the homeless and in the communal houses they shared with them. In fact, the basic ideology of the CWs as a group was to have direct contact with and provide hands-on support to individuals they sought to help. Many of the volunteers felt that interacting with the homeless and the community as a whole was invigorating. Chris describes how serving meals to the homeless was "uplifting" and created a "special bond" between him and the community in which he lived. These experiences reinvigorated the volunteers and kept them committed despite the intense demands placed on them within the groups and the long hours they worked.

In contrast, members of CWA and the HA did not interact with a constituency they were aiming to help. The focus of CWA and the HA was policy, and these groups sought social change on the scale of national and municipal institutions, respectively. These organizations lacked a group of individuals to whom they could give help firsthand and with whom they could interact face-to-face. As a result, their focus was primarily on elites or individuals who were potential recruits to their organization (other conservative Protestant women or homeowners within their city). These foci made it difficult to foster the type of commitment that results from seeing the immediate consequences of one's activism for specific individuals. Over time, this contributed to the waning commitment of individuals in these groups.

Social Ties after Disengagement

It is clear that many individuals develop social ties through the course of participating in a social movement organization. In organizations that are communal, that involve joint engagement in ritual activity, and that facilitate interaction between members and constituents, it is more likely that these ties will be created and sustained. Some members may maintain these ties even after leaving the social movement in which they were created. In general, I find that the stronger the ties are during engagement, the more likely individuals are to maintain those ties even after they leave the group, if they do so. In addition, Table 9 demonstrates that having more ties with members after disengagement from the original group, if that occurred, made it more likely that individuals would either follow an abeyance trajectory or transfer to another group instead of disengaging from participation permanently.[6] I examine each of the four groups in turn to delineate the factors that make groups more or less able to foster these types of enduring ties and, consequently, facilitate the lasting engagement of their members even if they temporarily leave a group.

The Catholic Workers were very successful at maintaining ties between current and past members. Seventy-nine percent (11 of 14) of the individuals who left the group stayed in contact with other CW members. The annual Solstice Festival and the monthly potluck dinners, described earlier, were two events that worked to keep current and past members in contact with one another. These events were significant because they facilitated the reengagement of individuals even if they had left the group over time. Individuals who stayed in contact through the festival and potluck dinners were more likely to engage in abeyance or transfer rather than to disengage from participa-

Table 9 Interaction with fellow participants after disengagement from focal group by group

Group	Interaction postparticipation	Trajectory		
		Disengage (%) (N = 27)	Abeyance (%) (N = 9)	Transfer (%) (N = 15)
Catholic Workers	Yes (N = 11)	9	27	64
	No (N = 3)	66	33	—
Concerned Women for America	Yes (N = 0)	—	—	—
	No (N = 11)	91	—	9
United Farm Workers	Yes (N = 7)	14	43	43
	No (N = 3)	66	—	33
Homeowners Association	Yes (N = 3)	—	33	66
	No (N = 12)	92	—	8
TOTAL	Yes (N = 22)	10	33	57
	No (N = 29)	86	4	11

NOTES: Fisher's exact test is significant at p-value < 0.001.

Individuals who persisted in their participation are excluded for this table. Ten individuals persisted in total.

tion permanently. In fact, 91 percent (10 of 11) of the CW members with post-participation ties reengaged in participation, while only 33 percent (1 of 3) of those without such ties did so. Daniel, a priest who transferred from the CW community to another social justice group in the area, describes his relationships with other past CW members in the following way:

> We are as close as a family that can see each other four or five times a year and it is like there has been no separation. It is that close. I can still walk into anyone's house and open the refrigerator and see if there is any beer, which is friendlier than I am with some of my brothers and sisters.

Arnold notes that when he "think[s] of friends in the neighborhood, even though timewise I don't get to see these people anywhere near what I would like, I still think of the [CW] community of people as my friendship base in the neighborhood."

These ties provided the basis for later participation, such as when a group of past CW volunteers came together after September 11, 2001, to form a social justice group. This group was focused on raising awareness of potential problems with American foreign policy abroad, highlighting racism within the United States, and mobilizing against a potential war. These individuals, led by a judge who had been a longtime member of the CW community, used the CW house as the base for organization and mobilization. Being tied to other participants made this new mobilization more likely, and individuals with these types of ties were more likely to engage in social movement activities later in life.

Postparticipation ties were also important for the United Farm Workers. The strong friendships that were created through the intensive interaction at La Paz were often maintained long after individuals left the group. Seventy percent (7 of 10) of the UFW participants maintained these ties even after they left the group. Charlie describes his relationships with other past volunteers as based on a common bond:

> It is like you served in the trenches of a war and you have these war buddies. You have a common experience that is so intense that you can talk to that buddy many many years or decades later and you have this common ground or experience that you can call on to talk about.

Sylvia notes that her "true friends in the movement are still her best friends even after 38 years." These strong ties led many of the activists to move to another social justice group or engage in abeyance by leaving and then reengaging in participation later in life. Among the UFW participants, 86 percent (6 of 7) of those who kept in touch with other past volunteers reengaged in participation later in life, while only 33 percent (1 of 3) of those without such ties did so.

The members of the Concerned Women for America and the Homeowners Association were much less likely to maintain ties if they disengaged. In fact, none of the CWA members maintained ties after they left the group, while only 20 percent (3 of 15) of the HA did so. The lack of strong ties created in both CWA and the HA, partly because of the lack of interaction among members, made it less likely that individuals kept in touch after leaving their group. Those who had fewer postparticipation ties were more likely to completely withdraw from activism.

Discussion and Conclusion

Social ties and interaction are clearly important parts of the process whereby individuals come to participate in social movements and contentious politics. In this chapter, I examine how ties are fostered within organizations and help to keep individuals active over time. Elements of organizational structure, including the level of hierarchy in the group and the amount of interaction in the organization, have a significant effect on the number and intensity of social bonds created in the course of participation. In turn, the social ties created within organizations impact the trajectory of an individual's participation in social movements.

Almost all of the individuals interviewed became involved in a social movement organization through social ties. In all four groups, those individuals who had personally known a rank-and-file member before they became involved with the group were more likely to stay involved. However, not all individuals knew or were recruited by rank-and-file members. Many individuals in hierarchical groups were recruited by organizational leaders and, as a result, were less likely to stay involved in the group over time, although this effect can be somewhat mitigated by the level of interaction the new recruits had with leaders once in the group.

In the UFW, many new participants were mobilized by movement leaders, and then these individuals were in regular contact with these leaders in the course of their participation. This was not the case in CWA: while many individuals in CWA were recruited by leaders, there was virtually no subsequent interaction. This lack of interaction with one's recruiter led to less persistent participation over time. Thus there is an interactive effect between recruiter and level of interaction that then predicts an individual's trajectory of participation.

Social movements often involve intensive interaction in the course of participation, but this is not always the case. In communal groups that involve high levels of interaction and joint engagement in ritual activity, the bonds between people become stronger, keeping members active over time. In addition, interaction with the constituency one aims to help, such as the homeless or farm workers, can keep participants motivated to persist in their engagement despite demanding and difficult conditions.

Finally, individuals who leave a particular SMO may maintain social ties with others with whom they were previously active. Those who have stronger ties while in social movements are more likely to sustain those ties even after they leave. Some groups are more effective at sustaining these types of postengagement ties. The CWs, for example, hold festivals and monthly potlucks that keep past members connected to one another and to the group, even if they are no longer actively participating. These postengagement ties make individuals more likely to engage in abeyance or transfer to another group rather than disengage from participation altogether.

In this chapter, I outlined the role of social ties in social movement participation. In addition to social ties, an individual's identity also affects his trajectory of participation over time. Identities that support participation may be solidified by social ties. The next chapter examines the creation of these identities in the four movement contexts and assesses the effect of these identities on the length and continuity of individual participation.

6 We Are Not All Activists

The Development and Consequences of Identity

WHEN ASKED WHY SHE THINKS some people stay politically active while others do not, Eileen, a 14-year member of the Catholic Workers, succinctly says, "I think it depends on the extent to which people understand their identity as being a member of something like that or not." Eileen's explanation highlights not only that identities are important precipitants of joining a social movement—something that has long been recognized—but also that they are important consequences of participating and predictors of continued engagement over time.

Identities are fundamentally relational and developed through reciprocal interaction with others (Tilly 2005; Stekelenburg and Klandermans 2007). Eileen, for example, describes how being a member of the CW was "part of [her] identity. Maybe it is a part of an identity I chose and cultivated as opposed to just had." For Eileen and other participants like her, identities emerge through organizational participation. They are created by the participants themselves in an interactive, shared process, "constructed and negotiated by repeated activation of the relationship that links individuals to the group" (Melucci 1995, 44).

Much of the work on social movements and identity finds that individuals who are engaged in social movements and contentious politics come to identify as activists, and they see this identity as highly salient (see, e.g., Teske 1997). This finding is based primarily on case studies of leftist movements involving high levels of commitment, such as the civil rights, antiwar, and women's movements. Not all individuals come to identify in this way, however. In fact, I show that the identity individuals develop is shaped both by the organizational context in which they engage and by individual personal characteristics. In particular, the issue scope of the organization as a whole, ranging from a focus on a single issue to a concern with a broader multiplicity of issues, affects the identities individuals develop within the group. In addition, individual characteristics, such as one's political ideology and past experience with contentious politics, also shape one's identity development.

As the preceding chapter has highlighted, sustained interaction among movement members is critical for creating a sense of community. Building on this insight, this chapter illuminates how identities develop through participation in a movement. I show that not all participants who engage in an SMO (social movement organization) or protest activity identify as activists; individuals engaging in the same behaviors, such as protesting, writing letters, and meeting with other participants, may come to identify in different ways. On the basis of the interview data as well as previous theoretical work, I delineate three general types of identities that can be developed in the course of movement participation: an activist identity, an organizational identity, and a value identity. Furthermore, I show that the type of identity one develops matters for future participation—one's identity affects how long one remains in a group, whether one is likely to transfer to another group, and whether one is likely to follow an abeyance pattern of participation. Accordingly, it is not the contentious political behaviors, but the ways in which individuals make sense of these behaviors and identify themselves, that have consequences for their future engagement.

Identity

Identities are the names that people give to themselves and others in the course of social interaction (Snow 2001). Individuals have many identities, which are organized according to their subjective importance and salience, or how readily they are invoked in a situation (Stryker and Serpe 1994). These identities allow individuals to locate themselves within the world and act accordingly. Collective identities are central to social movement participation—these identities provide a sense of "we-ness" or "one-ness" that derives from perceived shared attributes or experiences among those who comprise a group (Melucci et al. 1989). Some sociologists argue that a collective identity is a prerequisite for collective action (Klandermans and de Weerd 2000). Others find that social movement engagement leads participants to fundamentally change their identities and the way they see themselves (Rupp and Taylor 1987; Taylor and Raeburn 1995; Whittier 1995). Thus identities can either precipitate or result from social movement participation.

Identities may take a variety of forms in the course of an individual's engagement in SMOs or activities. Gamson (1991) posits that movement collective identities have three embedded levels. First, there is the organizational activist identity that is specific to a particular SMO. Second, there is the broader movement activist identity, which may be sustained over time as individuals move from one organization to another.[1] Finally, individuals may experience a collective identity based on social categories, such as ethnicity or community of residence. To illustrate, a member of the United Farm Workers might identify with that specific organization, with the labor movement as a whole, or with an ethnic group such as Latino. The relative salience, or importance, of each of these identities can shift over time and is dependent on the context.

In addition to these three embedded levels of collective identity, individuals can also develop what Gecas (2000) refers to as a value identity, which can become an important part of an individual's overall sense of self. Values have a wide range of identity implications, such as telling individuals who they are, where they fit into the social hierarchy, who is a member of their community and who is not, and how individuals should relate to authority (Warren 1990). In effect, they provide a moral framework for social relations and individual experience.

In combination, the work of Gamson (1991) and Gecas (2000) outlines the variety of identities individuals can develop in the course of social movement participation. Despite these theoretical developments, recent work in this area has been slow to apply these ideas and examine the diversity of identities that can result from social movement participation and the mechanisms that lead to the formation of different identities. This chapter builds on these important theoretical contributions by examining the variety of identities that individuals developed in four SMOs. This comparison illustrates that social movement participation does not inevitably result in the adoption of one particular type of identity. In fact, I show that individuals engaging in different organizational contexts and with different past experiences and ideologies vary in their propensity to identify as organizational members, with the values of the group, or as activists. I seek to understand, first, how and why individuals identify differently and, second, the implications of these different identities for participation over time.

Identity Development: The Role of Organizational Structure

Identities are fluid and develop as individuals interact with one another in social groups. Given the variety of possible identities, what explains which identity or identities an individual will adopt in the course of participating in contentious politics? In this analysis, I examine the role of issue scope within an organization and an individual's personal history and ideology in the development of identity within social movements.

As discussed in Chapter 4, SMOs differ in the extent to which they focus on one specific issue or a larger set of beliefs. Many social movements are based on ideologies that join together a number of beliefs. For example, the Catholic Workers and the Concerned Women for America offer holistic ideologies of social justice and conservative Protestant Christianity, respectively. These overarching ideologies are tied to a number of specific issues, such as resisting war and helping the homeless, in the case of the CW. CWA focuses primarily on opposition to gay marriage, sex education, and abortion, seeing these issues as broadly reflective of conservative Protestant Christianity.

However, not all SMOs agree on a wide range of interconnected issues and beliefs. In fact, many SMOs are founded on one specific issue. Individuals in these groups often express very high levels of commitment to these specific issues and beliefs, but the organization or its leaders do not present them as connected to other issues. The United Farm Workers and the Homeowners Association are based on agreement on a narrower set of issues. The UFW works to promote the rights of farm workers but tends not to get involved in other issues on the political left, such as antiwar mobilization or women's rights. Similarly, the HA actively attempts to restrict the number of homeless individuals in their city but do not mobilize around other related causes.

In this analysis I compare what I label "single-issue" groups with "multi-issue" groups. Multi-issue groups are groups that work on at least two issues that they see as connected to a larger, overarching ideology. Single-issue groups work for one specific cause and do not explicitly tie this cause to other issues. I argue that the issue scope of an SMO affects the identities participants develop over time.

Activist Identity

Past studies of SMOs tend to find that individuals who become involved in these groups define themselves as activists and feel this identity to be highly salient. As demonstrated in Figure 8, however, I find that the connection be-

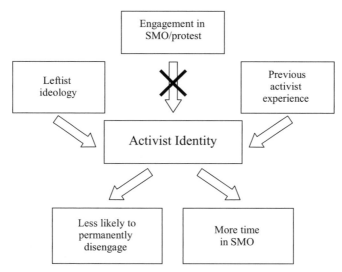

Figure 8 Predictors and consequences of an activist identity. The relationship indicated by an arrow with an X through it is presumed in the literature but does not always exist.

tween engagement in social movement activities or groups and having an activist identity is not automatic; not all individuals who engage in social movements come to see this as activism or to define themselves in this way. In fact, two individuals can engage in the same behaviors, such as meeting with other participants, petitioning, protesting, and lobbying, and only one of them will develop an activist identity. I seek to understand why these same behaviors come to be understood in different ways as well as the effects of an activist identity on the continuity of social movement participation over time.

Generally, individuals who are leftist in ideology and who participated in social movement activities before their involvement in the SMOs in this analysis are more likely to define themselves as activists. Individuals who define themselves as activists remain in their SMO for longer periods and are less likely to disengage permanently from activism if they leave their group. The independent sample t-tests, reported in Table 10, demonstrate these findings. These findings highlight how individual experiences and characteristics can significantly affect social movement engagement. When examining participants in all four groups together, individuals who describe themselves as leftists and have past social movement experience are more likely to define themselves as activists.

Not all individuals, however, are equally likely to define themselves as

Table 10 Independent sample t-tests between select variables and the presence of an activist identity and participation

	Activist identity (1 = activist identity)	Disengaged permanently (1 = disengaged permanently)	Years in focal group
Previous social movement participation (1 = past participation)	1.309*	—	—
Leftist ideology (1 = leftist ideology)	10.650**	—	—
Define self as activist (1 = define as activist)	—	−4.361**	−3.452**

NOTE: Cells contain t-scores from the independent sample t-test.
*Significant at the 0.1 level.
**Significant at the 0.001 level.

leftists or have previous social movement experience. These features are related to the organization in which they are involved. Because these two factors predict the development of an activist identity and, consequently, affect long-term participation in social movements, it is important to examine these variables in each of the four group contexts. Through the use of the interview data, it is possible to examine why and how being a leftist and having past social movement experience lead to the development of an activist identity and how that, in turn, makes continued engagement more likely.

Individuals in both the Catholic Workers and the United Farm Workers are far more likely to have been involved in other SMOs prior to joining these groups. As shown in Table 11, 80 percent (12 of 15) of the CWs and 87 percent (13 of 15) of the UFW members had been involved in other SMOs. Many UFW members, for example, had previous social movement experience in college or university, where they joined groups such as MEChA or other Latino or farm worker–based groups. Other UFW volunteers had parents who took them to protests and strikes when they were young. Anthony, a 59-year-old union organizer, said that he was "kind of born into the movement. . . .I was born to parents who were community activists in the 1940s." His father belonged to a group of Latino men who advocated for Mexican American rights in Los Angeles and his mother was a leader of a community service organization.

The CWs were less likely to have come from activist families. In fact, most CW members came from families that were conservative or Catholic and did little in the way of social activism. For individuals in this group, it was more often a transformative experience in college or university that provided the basis for subsequent engagement. Arnold, for example, was raised in a conservative Catholic family. He went to a very leftist liberal arts college and became involved in Students for a Democratic Society (SDS) on campus. Through this group he became involved in a summer union-organizing group and, later, the CW. His engagement in college laid the foundation for his later participation in the CW community. Anthony, Arnold, and most other UFW and CW members' past experiences made them more likely to self-define as activists.

In addition, the CW and UFW members all held leftist values and viewed engagement in contentious politics and activism in a positive light.[2] Among these individuals, activism was seen as a productive way to deal with troubling historical events and social problems. For example, Phil, a CW member, describes how the infamous Kent State shootings in 1970 pushed him to become involved in what he defined as activism, instead of volunteering or community service:

> When I was in high school, I was not politically active. We did some volunteer projects with church groups and things like that. And when I got to college, it became more important but it was still probably primarily sort of service kinds of activities. Tutoring little kids and stuff like that. Until Kent State, and then everything became real politicized and everything became more movement-oriented and change-oriented and more political. *I became an activist at that point, instead of just a volunteer.* (emphasis added)

Other CW members talked about how the Vietnam War spurred them to politicized activism. Sean served in the military in the Second World War and was shot down while on duty. Later, at the start of the Vietnam War, Sean became an antiwar activist through the Catholic Peace Movement, including the CW community. Sean saw his antiwar activism as a positive way to deal with what he characterized as a troubling historical development in American foreign policy.

As a result of these positive definitions of activism, all individuals in the UFW and CW defined themselves as activists and saw this as an important part of their identity. Chris, a 53-year-old social worker in the CW, told me that being an "activist is just who I am, it is in my blood." Other group members talked about how being an activist was "part of [their] identity" or a part of their "sense of self." This activist identity helped tie together the diverse membership in these groups. For example, the UFW brought together people from a variety of different ethnic and racial groups that historically had

Table 11 Factors leading to the development of an activist identity by group

	Catholic Workers		Concerned Women for America		United Farm Workers		Homeowners Association	
	No "activist" identity	"Activist" identity	No "activist" identity	"Activist" identity	No "activist" identity	"Activist" identity	No "activist" identity	"Activist" identity
Factors								
Previous social movement participation		80% (12)		0% (0)		87% (13)		20% (3)
Leftist ideology*		100% (0)		0% (0)		100% (15)		53% (8)
Outcome								
Define self as activist		100% (15)		0% (0)		100% (15)		13% (2)
Trajectory								
Persistence	—	7% (1)	27% (4)	—	—	33% (5)	—	—
Transfer	—	47% (7)	7% (1)	—	—	27% (4)	23% (3)	50% (1)
Abeyance	—	27% (4)	—	—	—	20% (3)	0% (0)	—
Disengagement	—	20% (3)	67% (10)	—	—	20% (3)	77% (10)	50% (1)

*Operationalized as Democrat/Green political party identification, as opposed to Republican/Libertarian party identification.

organized separately with more limited success. As Valerie, a Filipino farm worker, explained:

> Another thing that Cesar did that was really important, the workers were al- ways really divided. You had Filipino crews, you had Mexican crews, you had Arab crews at one point. And my father is Filipino and my mother is Mexican so you have to deal with racism from both because you are not really Mexi- can and you are not really Filipino. But Cesar fought that and really brought us all together as [farm worker] activists and that was the first time that I felt I was in an environment where people would celebrate the workers and the Mexicans and the Filipinos working together as brothers and sisters together for a cause.

Valerie found that the broader activist identity enabled the bridging of indi- viduals from a variety of racial and ethnic groups. Because of this, the activ- ist identity "really embraced all that I am. That was powerful for me and im- portant for my children."

In contrast, members of the Concerned Women for America and the Homeowners Association did not generally identify as activists, nor did they define their participation in these groups as social movement activism. In fact, one interviewee insisted that I not call CWA an SMO, telling me that "we are not those radical protesters. We are a public policy group and we pray and we lobby. We are not the types to hold picket signs." Activism was seen as a negative thing in these groups because it was associated with leftist anti- Vietnam war protests and a lack of patriotism. As a whole, members of CWA defined their organization as a public policy group. Likewise, members of the HA did not describe their group as a social movement, choosing instead to call it a "neighborhood group," a "nonprofit group," or a "group about local politics."

Yet CWA and the HA did in fact engage in traditional social movement tactics, such as protesting and petitioning, despite my interviewees' claims to the contrary. The HA organized a series of protests at the local city hall to push for the passing of antipanhandling laws. Some CWA members protested outside abortion clinics. One member of CWA, Elizabeth, who did not con- sider herself to be politically active, participated in a "Gay Days" protest at the San Diego Zoo, a day when the zoo celebrates gay pride by explicitly wel- coming gay men and lesbians to the zoo. She did not see this as a form of pro- test, despite her account of standing with a group in solidarity and personally carrying a sign. This understanding of protest activity was typical of CWA and HA interviewees. Thus, it is not the specific behaviors in which one engages but the meaning one assigns to those behaviors that leads to the development of an activist identity. And this in turn affects patterns of future participation.

Organizations themselves help to shape how individuals view activism. In hierarchical, centralized groups such as CWA, the national organization is instrumental in framing the group as focused on public policy rather than as a social movement. Press releases and the monthly CWA newsletter are important in this process. The CWA leadership uses the monthly newsletter to outline the main issues of concern. In fact, some newsletters even contained form letters that individual members were encouraged to send to elected leaders and a list of addresses of the people to whom they should be delivered. The newsletter also lists specific actions and causes in which their members should become involved. For example, a March 1985 newsletter lists three "actions" for members to engage in: write to their representatives and senators to urge them to cosponsor a specific bill labeled the "Preborn Children's Civil Rights Act of 1985"; write to their representatives and senators to oppose pay equity studies, which CWA called "needless and expensive"; and send for a "Porn Packet" guide sheet and join the April 27 event to protest the availability of pornographic materials to children in neighborhood stores. Despite the fact that this last event was a protest specifically organized by CWA, these specific calls to action worked to frame the group and issues in a way that emphasized the policy-related aspects of the organization rather than a more grassroots "activist" characterization.

Most individuals in CWA and the HA had little if any prior social movement experience. No CWA members I interviewed had previously belonged to another SMO or related group, and only 20 percent (3 of 15) of the HA members had earlier participatory experiences.[3] For example, before joining CWA, Irene "was not politically motivated or politically connected at all. So, no, [CWA] was a first." This was also the case for Lynn, who explained how, prior to her involvement in the HA, she had participated in "larger issues but not political things. I tend to stay out of the political."

Members of both CWA and the HA cited family duties as restricting their ability and interest in participating earlier in their lives. The quantitative analyses presented in Chapters 2 and 3 support this finding and show that, while individuals with children are more likely to have ever engaged, they are less likely to be able to sustain their participation over time. For example, Anna, a member of the HA, told me that she was not active until her daughter was ten years old. Before that, her husband worked "a thousand hours a week and I was like a single parent. I was not doing anything until she went to school." HA members also mentioned that career demands made earlier participation difficult. As Polly describes: "I was active in nothing until after I retired. There was no time." Because of their lack of previous social movement experience and their rightist ideology, the members of CWA and the HA tended not to see themselves as activists. The only exceptions were two women participants of the HA who were very liberal and who had both been active in social movements prior to their involvement in this group.

In summary, individuals in the CW and the UFW are more likely to have been involved in social movements prior to their involvement in these groups and are more likely to consider themselves as leftists. In turn, individuals with these characteristics are more likely to define themselves as activists. As individuals in CWA and the HA do not possess these characteristics, they are less likely to see themselves as activists.

Previous movement experience and leftist ideology are *necessary* but not *sufficient* conditions leading to an activist identity in my sample. This relationship is clearly demonstrated by looking at the HA, the only group where some individuals identified as politically left and others as politically right. In this group, 20 percent (3 of 15) of the respondents had previous social movement experience and 53 percent (8 of 15) defined themselves as leftists. However, only 13 percent (2 of 15) of the sample defined themselves as activists. Both of the women who did define themselves as activists were leftists and had past social movement experience. In other words, just being a leftist or just having movement experience is not enough to lead to an activist identity; only the two characteristics in combination lead to this type of identity. For example, Lynn identifies as a Democrat but had never engaged in other groups before the HA. When she moved into the community, she was recruited by a neighbor and became a board member of the group. However, after six years she started working for pay and stopped engaging in social movement activities. She has never returned. For Lynn, simply identifying as a leftist was not, on its own, a sufficient condition for continued action.

Thinking of oneself as an activist is not merely a matter of semantics: identifying as an activist has important implications for individuals. The significance of the activist identity resides, as shown in Table 10, in the fact that individuals who define themselves as activists persist in their participation in the focal group for more years, on average ($t = 3.452$, $p < 0.001$). They are also significantly less likely to disengage permanently from social movements if they do leave the group in which they were originally involved ($t = -4.361$, $p < 0.001$). So, while many participants in these four groups engaged in similar activities, *it was participants' self-definition as an activist that predicted their propensity to sustain participation and not permanently disengage from social movements*, even if they left their original group.

Organizational and Value Identities

While social movement participants can come to identify as activists, they can also come to identify with their organizations (Gamson 1991) or with general values (Gecas 2000). I posit that the identities that participants adopt, either organizational or value based, are related to a key element of organizational structure—the group's issue scope.

SMOs differ in the extent to which they are based on one issue or an interconnected set of beliefs. Groups such as the Catholic Workers and Concerned Women for America tie together sets of beliefs: the ideology of social justice in the case of the CW and conservative Protestant Christianity for CWA. These larger beliefs lead individuals to become involved in a variety of issues that they view as related to the larger ideology. In contrast, groups such as the United Farm Workers and the Homeowners Association are based on a narrower set of issues that are not directly connected to other issues by the organization or its leaders. This makes it less likely that individuals will move from cause to cause over time. I examine each of these four group contexts in more detail.

For members of the multi-issue groups, the CW and CWA, an organizational identity was less salient than overarching value identifications. For example, Joanne, a stay-at-home mother and longtime participant in CWA, illustrates the importance of her value identity when she states:

> [Being in CWA] is very important to me, but *it is not who I am*. As far as who I am, who I am is wrapped up in who I am in my relationship with the Lord. What I do is just how I use the gifts and the talents He has given me. (emphasis added)

Such statements were common among members of CWA. In essence, CWA was just one way to express her commitment to her religious identity. If she could no longer participate in CWA, another organization could easily fulfill this same function for her. By defining herself through her relationship with God and viewing her participation in CWA as an expression of her commitment to this relationship, Joanne emphasizes the salience of a value identity, as opposed to an organizational identity.

Religious identity also came to the fore in CWA members' explanations of how they came to join the organization. Many women expressed an early reluctance to join the group. They felt that time spent in CWA would take away from what they considered their primary roles as wives and mothers. Sally, who later became the leader of her state chapter, describes how she struggled to decide whether or not to become the leader after being asked to do so by a woman from the national CWA office. In order to make this decision, she decided to "pray on it." She prayed for two months and still had not come to a decision.

> By January, I did not feel that I was being directed to either do it or not do it. And I prayed once more and said, "God, you have got to give me an answer. I am not telling them yes, I am not telling them no until I hear from you." And I turned on the radio and there was a religious program on about a pro-life group. And I realized, I need to do this—He wants me to do this.

Three other women whom I interviewed from CWA had similar experiences. One of these women, who also became a state leader, told me that she "felt clearly from the Lord that I needed to do my part by joining the group" and that "the Lord was calling me to be a part of this. I was just trying to be obedient, to do the best I knew of what God was telling me to do." These explanations of initial participation highlight the significance of religion in the lives of CWA participants.

Many CWA members emphasized how their participation in the group was related to other roles in their lives. Because of their conservative Protestant values, the CWA respondents commonly emphasized the significance of being wives and mothers. Members were concerned that outsiders would judge them unfavorably for spending large amounts of time working outside the home, taking them away from what they described as their primary duties as wives and mothers. The women made sense of this apparent contradiction by arguing that CWA, and their participation in the group, was in fact a vehicle for expressing their commitment to their private family roles.

This was the case for Virginia, who explains that she originally joined

CWA because she felt it would help her husband and family: "So I decided I would be a supporter. You know a wife is supposed to be a help to her husband and meet his needs and her family's needs. And that has always been my priority. And joining CWA was one way I met those needs." Helen also saw her participation in CWA as primarily a way to serve her husband and family. She was active for a year in the group until her husband died, and she told me that since her husband passed away, she no longer participates in the group. "Now that my husband died, I don't have to do anything as far as the community or anything else to uphold his image, which is a lot of it. Keeping a husband looking good is something a wife should do. But, he has been gone for nine years, so this has been kind of my retirement years." Helen's and Virginia's stories illustrate how participation in the group was a way to demonstrate their commitment to their roles as wives and mothers.

Individuals express the centrality, or salience, of their identities by invoking them. An individual's multiple identities are organized into a hierarchy of salience, and the salience of an identity helps determine which activities or actions an individual will chose to undertake (Callero 1985; Nuttbrock and Freudiger 1991; Stryker 1980; Stryker and Serpe 1994). By invoking the identity of wife and tying their participation in CWA to their identity as Christians, the women in CWA are expressing the salience and centrality of their family and religious identities.

Similarly, although the Catholic Workers felt connected to their community as a whole, they mostly identified with the overarching value of social justice. This was, in part, because the CWs worked on a wide variety of issues, often in coalition with members of other community groups. The borders of the CW community were, therefore, quite porous, as individuals interacted often with other groups focused on social justice outside of the explicit CW community. As one ex–Catholic Worker, who is now a participant in an environmental group, told me, being involved in social justice campaigns and the values that they are based on is "just a part of who I am. And, you can no more turn your back on it than one can on anything else that is really part of who one is." She felt that social justice was a "part of [her] identity." This was a very common sentiment, and many CWs talked about the significance of social justice work to their overall sense of self.

Individuals in the CW and CWA, groups that tied together a number of specific issues under a larger ideology, expressed a primary commitment to a value identity as opposed to an identity rooted in a specific organization. Thus these groups constituted contexts that were conducive to the creation of similar types of identity, despite the vast differences between the organizations in terms of structure and activities.

Individuals in these multi-issue groups are more likely to transfer to another organization if they disengage from the original group because the overarching ideology in these groups is attached to a variety of different specific issues. In the CW, as shown in Table 11, 47 percent (7 of 15) of past participants transferred to another social justice group after disengaging from the CW community. In CWA, while only 7 percent (1 of 15) shifted to another SMO, an additional 67 percent (10 of 15) transferred to participating in their churches. While these churches were not SMOs, as they did not engage in external activity to lobby government or power holders,[4] these organizations provided another means of expressing opinions that are consistent with conservative Protestant ideology.

Organizations such as the United Farm Workers and the Homeowners Association tended to focus on a narrower set of issues.[5] Members of the UFW, for example, generally express high levels of commitment to the goals of the group but tend to participate almost exclusively in issues related to farm workers, not engaging in other leftist causes. As a result, UFW participants tend to identify strongly with the organization itself. The leadership were the focus of considerable loyalty and respect, particularly Cesar Chavez, who was admired for his strong commitment to the organization itself and his personal sacrifices for the group. According to Sylvia, a 12-year participant of the UFW who now works for a UFW support group:

> [All the volunteers at La Paz] saw Cesar Chavez there voluntarily, an individual who lived in poverty voluntarily, being paid 5 dollars a week just like everyone else in the movement was. It wasn't based on money, it was based on commitment and sacrifice. And I think that people were really turned on that they could work for someone who was sacrificing as they were, versus someone who was making hundreds of thousands of dollars being the leader of something. It was different here. It started at the top.

Chavez's leadership by example is well known. This dedication was clear when Chavez himself said:

> If we're going to lead people and ask them to starve and to really sacrifice, we've got to do it first, do it more than anybody else. . . .I wanted [the leaders] to suffer with the strikers. I demanded full commitment. (Chavez, quoted in Levy 1975, 242)

Members' personal loyalty to Chavez translated into considerable organizational attachment, as well as a strong and salient organizational identity, for UFW activists.

The women involved in Concerned Women for America also expressed considerable personal attachment to, and admiration for, the national leader, Beverly LaHaye. This admiration, however, was based on her embodiment of conservative Protestant ideology rather than her devotion to the organization. One social worker, who left CWA after a short period, stated that "as a Christian person, Beverly was every single thing that I believed in." While this woman and many other participants were personally attached to LaHaye, clearly this attachment was based on her typification of conservative Protestant Christianity and not on her leadership of CWA. Thus, one 51-year-old stay-at-home mother who has disengaged from social movements said that she "still believe[s] in Beverly LaHaye, but I believe and support my church where I can become physically active in things."

The more issue-specific focus of the UFW and the HA translated into a lower propensity among participants to transfer to other groups over time. The UFW members, for example, generally expressed strong commitment to the work of the group and participated almost exclusively in farm worker–related issues. As a result, most individuals in this group either sustained their participation or left and returned to this same group later in life, engaging in an abeyance trajectory within the same organization. Transfer to other groups was less common, with only 27 percent (4 of 15) of the individuals following this trajectory.[6] It is apparent from the long periods of engagement among the UFW members I interviewed (an average of 18.33 years, ranging from 5 to 41 years) that commitment to the cause of farm workers was very strong.

Similarly, in the Homeowners Association, individuals were specifically committed to restricting the number and activities of the homeless and protecting homeowners' rights in their community. These issues were not tied to a larger, multi-issue agenda, such as improving schools, services, or representation in their city. They also did not identify strongly with the organization itself. This is made clear, in part, by the many name changes the group underwent. It is additionally a result of the ideological divide in the group, with 53 percent (8 of 15) identifying as Democrat and 47 percent (7 of 15) as Republican.

The ideological split in the group meant that it was not viable to create an extensive ideology; it simply would not have been acceptable to everyone in the group. This was clear when Diana described how she and Karen were able to work together despite the fact that she considered herself a staunch conservative whereas Karen is a strong Democrat.

> [Cooperation was possible because] we did not focus on the political. We were just interested in enforcing the law that people who live here and pay taxes here should have some sort of rights over people who want to harass you and graffiti your property and use the school yard for their personal potty. This cuts across the political spectrum. I might be harder lined than [Karen], but everyone within the group wanted the city to be what it had been.

This general framing of the cause of the group, focusing on things about which many people in the community agreed despite more nuanced ideological differences, enabled the group to function despite ideological divisions.

Because of the lack of a large and cohesive ideology tying the group to other causes, however, individuals who left the HA were unlikely to join other social movements. In fact, only 27 percent (4 of 15) of those who left this group engaged in another SMO later in life. As Diana described previously, this group was so focused on specific issues, such as getting the homeless out of the park, that individual members did not actively embrace a larger ideological frame that would support action in other groups or on behalf of other causes later in life. Only those who came to the group with a broader ideology went on to participate in other groups.

Discussion and Conclusion

Identities do not emerge automatically and in predetermined ways as a result of social movement engagement. Individuals participate in different organizational contexts, and with their disparate personal experiences and ideologies they differ in their propensity to identify as organizational members, with the values of the group, or as activists. My interview data show that, contrary to the assumptions of much past work, not all individuals who participate in SMOs and related activities define themselves as activists. In both the CW and the UFW, individuals tend to identify as activists and this identity is personally important for them. Most individuals in these two groups already had experience in social movements before their engagement in these organizations and saw themselves as leftist, both characteristics associated with a more positive attitude toward activism.

In CWA and the HA, on the other hand, individuals did not tend to define themselves as activists. Engagement in these groups was generally their first foray into social movement participation. Members were more likely to hold right-leaning political views. And so, they did not label their organization as part of a social movement, instead seeing themselves as a public policy or neighborhood group. The significance of the activist identity lies in the fact that individuals who identify as activists participated, on average, much longer than those who did not identify in this way.

Individuals in multi-issue organizations, organizations that offer a cohesive ideology bridging a variety of specific issues, are more likely to identify with a value identity than with the specific movement organization in which they participate. As a result, these individuals more often transfer to other groups because they see the interconnection of multiple issues consistent with their overall ideology. Individuals who engage in more issue-specific organizations are much less likely to transfer to other groups over time.

As Chapters 5 and 6 have shown, participants create social ties and identities within social movements that have important consequences for both the duration and continuity of their engagement. These chapters highlight the significance of the organizational and relational context of an individual's participation for shaping these ties and identities. Chapter 7, the concluding chapter, looks beyond organizational context and examines the effect of the historical period during which the individuals in this book participated to assess the role of this period in shaping their engagement.

7 Beyond the "Activist"

THINKING ABOUT CONTENTIOUS POLITICS brings to mind a very specific image of an "activist"—a lifelong participant, passionately committed to the cause. The role of such an activist has been well documented in a variety of campaigns, including those opposing slavery and the Vietnam War and those promoting suffrage and gay rights. Even when such campaigns face massive opposition, activists remain steadfast in their support and convictions. Whether they inspire applause or derision from others, activists persist in their commitment to their causes over time.

Despite the larger-than-life nature of this image, the lifelong, intensely committed, and passionate activist is far from typical. As I have argued throughout this book, the tendency to focus exclusively on persistent activists obscures contentious political participation in two main ways. First, rather than simply being the purview of a small group of extremely dedicated activists, contentious politics is an activity that is pursued by a large number of people; fully 65 percent of the respondents from the panel survey in this study have belonged to a social movement organization or participated in a protest event at least once in their lives.

Second, focusing on lifelong activists obscures the fluctuating and intermittent nature of most participants' engagement. While the stereotypical activist typically stays in the same group for a long period, many participants move in and out of organizations. In fact, approximately two-fifths of those in this study who have participated in contentious politics shifted from group to group, or even from cause to cause. An additional two-fifths of the participants in this study left engagement never to return. These findings show that most participants are not persistent activists but instead engage in a variety of different trajectories of engagement. The present analysis adds to our understanding of what happens to individuals after their initial engagement by conceptualizing social movement participation in terms of four proposed trajectories, leading to a fuller understanding of individuals' participatory experiences. Moreover, because individuals can be classified using this typology of trajectories, it is possible to assess the factors that predict the intermittent and shifting involvement in which many of them engage.

This study illustrates that any complete understanding of contentious political engagement must move beyond descriptions of the "activist" by considering the multiple ways in which individuals can participate. Achieving this goal requires a broader conceptualization of contentious politics, one that encompasses the variety of groups and activities in civil society that create or resist social change. In keeping with this conceptualization, I have presented quantitative findings that assess people's engagement in a diverse range of activities, including protests, demonstrations, rallies, and marches. These analyses have also considered a variety of organizational settings, ranging from local community groups to politically oriented civic organizations.

The selection of case studies presented in the qualitative chapters was also intentionally broad. I selected four groups to ensure variability and diversity, which allow for a more general understanding of how contentious political engagement operates. The groups presented in the case studies vary in terms of their organizational and relational contexts. The inclusion of groups that differ in issue scope, intensity of interaction, and degree of hierarchy makes possible a theoretical assessment of the effect of these factors on individual participation.

The Main Findings: A Summary

Conceptualizing contentious political engagement as being varied in terms of its form and continuity allows us to examine how individual participation occurs over the life course and how the vast majority of participants move in and out of social movements over time. Taken together, the panel data analyses and in-depth interviews give us several important insights into contentious political engagement over the life course. The quantitative analyses presented in Chapters 2 and 3 shed light on the predictors of who will engage and the pattern of their engagement. The qualitative analyses presented in Chapters 4, 5, and 6 illuminate the contextual and social-psychological factors that shape one's trajectory of participation over time. In combination, this multi-method approach creates a fuller picture of individual participation.

I begin by assessing the individual-level predictors of participation. First, ideological factors are key determinants of whether or not an individual will ever engage in contentious politics. For example, those who are leftists, religious, and/or efficacious are more likely to have participated in a social movement group or activity of protest. However, while these ideological influences are important for predicting whether or not individuals will participate, they tell us little about the continuity or trajectory of engagement. Therefore, while a sympathetic ideology is an important precursor to engagement, individuals who persist do not, in fact, differ ideologically from those who move in and out of engagement, or who disengage completely.

Instead, symbolic resources and biographical factors are the most important predictors of one's propensity to remain active over the life course. The symbolic resource of education, for example, has a positive effect on initial engagement and is strongly related to persisting or following an abeyance pattern of participation. Thus, education works either to keep individuals involved or to pull them back into participation after a lull in engagement. In contrast, while political knowledge is also a positive predictor of engagement at some point in the life course, higher levels of knowledge are not associated with persistent participation over time. In combination, the quantitative data presented in this book show that we cannot simply use what is known about how individual-level factors predict initial participation to posit how they will be associated with continued engagement.

Biographical changes are even more significant in shaping individual engagement over the life course. For example, individuals who are single are the most likely to participate in contentious political action, and marrying reduces one's ability to maintain participation over time. Child rearing, working, and aging are also significantly related to shifting in and out of engagement. In combination, cultural resources and biographical changes account for the shifting engagement of individuals over the life course.

This study also highlights the importance of the organizational and relational context in which individuals participate. Factors such as the ideological scope of an organization, an organization's level of interaction, and its degree of hierarchy affect the participation of individual members. In order to assess the roles of these factors, I have extended past work by comparing the predictors of trajectory of participation in a dimensional sample of four SMOs. My results show that elements of organizational structure can affect the social ties and identities created in the course of participation, which, in turn, either support or undermine the continued engagement of members.

Social ties have long been recognized as important precursors to participation in SMOs. My in-depth interviews underscore this point—95 percent of the participants came to their SMOs through social ties. I show, however, that the type of social tie on which recruitment was based has important consequences for the length and continuity of individual participation. In all four groups, individuals recruited by a rank-and-file member were more likely to persist. In contrast, many individuals in the more hierarchical groups were recruited by organizational leaders and were less likely to stay involved in the group. This effect was mitigated to some extent by the subsequent level of interaction that new recruits had with leaders; when individuals interact with the leader who recruits them, they are less likely to disengage over time.

Social movements often involve intensive interaction in the course of participation, but this is not always the case. In communal groups that involve high levels of interaction and joint engagement in ritual activity, individuals strengthen their bonds with one another and tend to stay involved over time or reengage after a lull in participation. Social ties with past members can work to maintain the identity and the ideology that originally supported participation and thus encourage the reengagement of past participants with other, similar groups later in life.

The interviews conducted with past activists show that the identities participants develop in the course of engagement are shaped by the group's organizational context. Individuals in multi-issue organizations, for example, which offer a cohesive ideology bringing together a variety of specific issues, are more likely to identify with that ideology than with the specific movement organization in which they participate. As a result, these individuals often transfer to other groups because of the connection between the specific issues of those groups and a larger interconnected set of beliefs. In addition, not all individuals who participate in SMOs and protest activities define themselves as activists; individuals who have past social movement experience and are leftists are more likely to define themselves in this way. The significance of the activist identity lies in the fact that individuals who identify in this way participate, on average, for more years and are less likely to disengage than are those who do not identify in this way. These findings demonstrate the role of organizational structure in shaping the social ties and identities of participants, which, in turn, affect their trajectory of participation over time.

Implications for Protest over Time

Social movements follow cycles and are marked by phases of heightened conflict and contention across the social system (Tarrow 1996). One of the central themes guiding the analyses presented in this book is that, while individual participation cannot be understood without situating it in its political and social context, the rise and fall of movements as a whole is contingent on the shifting engagement of individual members. In this way, it is essential that any theoretical examination of social movements also recognize that it is individual decisions to stay with or leave contentious political activity that ultimately determine whether campaigns and organizations succeed or fail.

Participant decisions to leave groups are related both to individual life circumstances and to the organizational context of engagement. For example, as discussed earlier, marrying and having children can suppress participation and lead to disengagement. In addition, individuals in organizations with limited member interaction and a narrow issue scope are less likely to persist or follow an abeyance pattern of participation.

However, an individual's decision to join or leave a movement is also affected by the external political environment. Regardless of people's commitment to an issue, they are more likely to engage when they think they will be effective, and there are certain contexts that make this more likely. Also, issues are more salient at certain times because of the social and political context, and individuals should be more likely to join groups at these times. For example, people who are concerned with resisting war are more likely to participate in social movements and protest when there is an imminent risk of war, when the issue is most pressing and there are more opportunities for engagement.

Core activists are less affected by changes in the political context and larger cycles of protest because of a higher level of commitment, which makes them less vulnerable to the temptation to leave when times are difficult, such as when campaigns are demanding or have limited success. Such core activists are members who are more tightly connected to their groups because of strong and salient ties. These activists, however, are not evenly distributed across groups. For example, the Catholic Worker community examined in this book has a large group of core members who remained active over time. Many members were married to other CWs, lived communally with other families who were also actively involved in the CW community, and had jobs that were supportive of their continued engagement in the group. Such individuals were much less likely to leave the CW community, even during periods when the group experienced little immediate success and when the political context was less conducive to mobilization, because their lives were intertwined with their activism.

In contrast, Concerned Women for America has relatively few core members. On the whole, the women in this group who were interviewed for this study did not know other CWA members, and their spouses and families were rarely involved in the group. In addition, obligations to husbands and children worked as countervailing ties for many CWA members. While having a spouse inside the group helped to keep CWs involved over time, counterpressures from husbands and children outside CWA often pulled members of that group away from the organization. Additionally, the active involvement of most CWA members in their churches provided a viable alternative for their free time. For these reasons, there were fewer individuals in CWA who were core members and tightly connected to this group, and as a result more members of this group disengaged over time.

This study also highlights the effects of different social movements on one another. In particular, the transfer trajectory outlined in this book illuminates the microprocesses involved in social movement diffusion and spillover. Through the process of social movement spillover, one movement comes to affect another through shared personnel (Meyer and Whittier 1994). This sharing of personnel allows for a diffusion of tactics and frames from one organization to another, in part because "innovation is communicated through certain channels over time among members of a social system" (Rogers 1983, 14). This spillover from one group to another is related to the transfer trajectory followed by many participants in this book. For example, two UFW members were, at one time, members of CW communities.[1] In addition, three members of the CW community in this analysis participated in UFW-sponsored mobilization and engaged in strikes, boycotts, and marches with this group. And one member of the Homeowners Association explicitly mentioned her earlier experience with the grape boycotts, a significant campaign of the UFW.

There are certain individual characteristics and organizational contexts that make transfer more likely. For example, transferring is more common for individuals who identify with a larger ideology, as opposed to one specific organization. It is also related to social ties with members in other groups and the extent to which the organization in which one engages has porous boundaries and works in coalition with other organizations. Knowing who transfers from group to group and why they do so can help us to understand the ways in which movement organizations affect one another.

Both the panel and interview data capture the experiences of a specific cohort of individuals who came of age in a period in the United States that is sometimes referred to as the protest era. The primary advantage of studying individuals who came of age in this period, and who initially participated in the social movements of the 1970s and 1980s, is that a multitude of trajectories of participation and a large portion of the life cycle can be documented. Nevertheless, there are a number of ways in which this period of engagement likely affected the participation of this cohort and therefore the findings of this study.

There is no question that over the past 50 years there have been radical changes in the character of protest in modern industrial democracies, including the United States. First, since the 1960s and 1970s there has been an increase in the frequency of protest events, as well as in levels of individual participation in protest activity (Meyer and Tarrow 1998). In the United States, the percentage of people who have participated in a demonstration increased from 11 percent in 1975 to 21 percent in 1999. Moreover, this trend is not unique to the United States—during the last quarter of the twentieth century, most advanced industrial democracies have seen a rise in protest participation (Inglehart 1997; Norris 2002).

Second, not only has the frequency of protest increased but its character has also changed fundamentally. On the one hand, protest is now a more varied and ubiquitous feature of modern society. Thus, it is utilized with greater frequency, involves a more varied set of tactics, is employed by a more diverse constituency, and is used to advocate for a wider range of claims. On the other hand, modern protest is also professionalized and institutionalized. This makes it more routinized and less contentious than it has been in the past. In essence, modern protest is more reformist than the revolutionary protests of the 1960s and 1970s. These changes have had real consequences for the individuals in this study—individuals who initially engaged in protest in one context but who now live in an environment in which protest is decidedly different. How did the individuals in this study, who participated in protest and social movements over time, experience this transition?

It has been long believed that individuals become more conservative as they age. It is also assumed that while young radicals engage in protest, these same people moderate with age, because concerns with family, finances, and their futures increasingly occupy their attention. If these hypotheses are true, perhaps individuals who themselves are becoming more conservative with age would welcome the more conventional and less disruptive tactics that became popular in the 1980s and beyond. They may also embrace the new set of issues that became the focus of protest activity, including an array of issues on the political right. If the individual protesters themselves were becoming more mainstream, the moderating nature of protest would constitute a compatible evolution over time.

As we know from other studies, however, individuals who engaged in the social movements of the 1960s and 1970s tended to remain relatively consistent in their beliefs (see e.g., Fendrich 1993; Jennings and Niemi 1981; McAdam 1988; Whalen and Flacks 1989). This consistency over time is also reflected in my data. When Neal, who now leads a large charitable organization, describes the future lives of the other Catholic Workers with whom he was active in the 1970s, he says:

> I can't think of anybody that left the [CW] community that is now doing something totally different, who is now in the corporate offices of Bank of America or something. Everybody seems to still be involved to some degree or another. One of the founders became a judge for a while, but he was a judge in a housing court, trying to deal with some very tough urban issues. So, I think even people who left the [CW] find other ways to express their ideology—an ideology that remains pretty much the same over time.

While the members of the cohort in this study might not have moderated their political views over time, they have nonetheless experienced major life changes. Aging, marriage, the birth of children, and career constraints would have been significant burdens, even for those individuals who remained clearly dedicated to their causes. As individuals in this cohort aged and experienced these life-cycle changes, the rise of more conventional and less revolutionary tactics might have been a welcome option for those who were now less biographically available in terms of time and the ability to take risks for the movement. While many individuals might have been willing to accept the risks of arrest or physical harm when they were single and not working, they may have been less likely to take these risks as they aged, regardless of their commitment to and interest in their causes.

This was certainly the case for Cynthia, who worked as a UFW lawyer for 22 years. For part of this time she lived and worked at La Paz, but she later moved to San Diego where she continued to work for the union. Cynthia describes how she ended up transferring out of the UFW and yet remained committed to farm worker issues:

> I wanted to continue helping people and I particularly wanted to focus on farm workers. But, I knew I had a responsibility as a parent to two children and I didn't feel like I could do justice to either at that point. And in terms of what I do here [at the volunteer legal aid center], a good percentage of my practice deals with farm worker issues. I have sued the city and I have sued slumlords and out of it we have gotten farm worker housing. So I am continuing in the same tradition, just now maybe I am dealing more with the personal legal needs of the farm worker population.

Thus, despite the changes owing to the birth of children, Cynthia was able to stay active in the movement by shifting the types of activities in which she engaged. In this way, as movement tactics became, on the whole, less risky and time intensive, individuals in this cohort might have been able to sustain their participation longer than would have been possible if the character of protest had remained the same over time.

Organizations can also adapt so as to facilitate the continued engagement of individuals who are experiencing biographical changes. This organizational adaptation could help groups to retain members over time, something that is critical for organizational survival. Turnover is difficult for organizations. When members leave groups, new members need to be found to replace them—a costly activity for the organization in terms of both time and energy. In addition, if new recruits are going to remain active over time, they have to be socialized into the group. At some point, if too many members leave or too few new members join, an organization may cease to exist. Because organizational maintenance is a core concern of SMO leaders and members, how can groups encourage the sustained participation of their members over time? This book provides some insight into this question.

First, intensive interaction facilitates the creation of social ties within groups, and these ties lead to longer participation and the continued commitment of individuals to organizations and causes over time. Therefore, organizations should work to foster these types of ties. Establishing a communal environment where members live and work together is a strategy that an organization can employ to manage this difficult task. But even if a fully communal environment cannot be created, encouraging interaction among members and between members and leaders can create bonds of solidarity in the group that encourage individuals to persist in their participation over time. In addition, staying in touch with past members who have left the organization makes it more likely that they will join other causes or return to the group later in life. The creation of these types of ties runs counter, in some ways, to the general trend of organizations, which are becoming more institutionalized and professionalized. However, groups that work to foster these types of bonds are more likely to facilitate the continued engagement of their members over the long term.

Social ties can also be useful in helping individuals deal with biographical impediments to participation. Having children, for example, can curtail engagement in contentious politics. Organizations that involve strong ties between members can help to overcome these problems. For example, having people available to watch children when members are engaging in social movement activities can make continued engagement possible for parents. In addition, organizations can incorporate child rearing into their social movement framing. Whether a group is on the political left or right, having children can make most issues seem more pressing and salient. Concerned Women for America, for example, made an explicit linkage between having families and the consequent necessity of protecting what they see as "traditional family values." Organizations that make this connection can help to encourage the persistence of their members even after they have children.

While the changing nature of protest in the period of this study was compatible with the life-cycle changes that many organizational members were facing, this change also led to some discontent. This occurred, in part, because of the changing levels of efficacy felt by many participants over time. When they initially engaged in protest in the 1960s and 1970s, many participants expressed an intense feeling of efficacy and optimism that their actions would lead to widespread social change. As Kevin, a persistent UFW volunteer, recounted:

> At the age of 25 I thought that if you put so many people together shoulder to shoulder and we threw all of our energy into this, we would eradicate racism, poverty, and social injustice over our lifetime. I really believed this, I am not making this up.

These feelings were echoed by David, another longtime UFW volunteer. David left university to join the union at the personal invitation of Cesar Chavez.

He told me, "I took a degree in history, I loved history. I loved reading about it and, at a certain point, after I met Cesar and got to know him, I kind of figured out that it would be a lot more interesting to be a part of history and not just to read about it." Sylvia expressed a similar point of view: "We didn't know we couldn't do it. That was the point. I didn't know I couldn't do it. Because Cesar always made you feel so powerful and so smart."

The sentiments felt by some movement participants, particularly those in leftist movements such as the UFW and the CW, were almost intoxicating. These groups gave the members a sense of personal power and agency that many found difficult to duplicate or sustain later in life. Charlie, who now works in a nonprofit fund-raising organization but continues to be active with the UFW, describes how involvement in later causes was difficult "because there is nothing that I could ever come across again after that experience [living and working at La Paz] that would be as intense and all demanding. First of all, it didn't exist. If you want to talk about joining other causes or a political party, it was never as intense or came close to the life I led in the farm worker movement."

In fact, many individuals I interviewed expressed a sense of disillusionment with the more moderate and conventional protest tactics of later periods. While it is clear that the institutionalization of social movement causes and issues that occurred in the 1980s, 1990s, and later was a partial success, it is also clear that this institutionalization involved some cooptation of more revolutionary ideas and causes. Future research should investigate the ways in which the cohort that came of age in the "protest era" were able or unable to adapt their participation to this changing social movement terrain.

A Modern Replication

What is the effect of the changing character and frequency of protest over time on the findings of this study? How would the findings of this study be different if they were based on a cohort of individuals who graduated from high school this year? Future work should examine how the participation of current high school seniors might differ from the experiences of the cohort presented in this book. Although we do not have such data at this stage, it is possible to offer some speculations or expectations. First, it is clear that the stereotype of the 1960s and 1970s as a time of very high levels of protest is somewhat misleading. While the protest events during that period might have been more dramatic than in previous times, protest levels in the United States and other modern industrial democracies are considerably higher today. For this reason, we would expect that, if this study were repeated with a current cohort of high school seniors, the overall levels of protest participation would be higher. This seems likely not only because more protest events take place today but also because the act of engaging in protest is less stigmatized than it was during the 1960s and 1970s.

In addition to the higher levels of protest, there are also many more issues and campaigns now than there were in the past. This trend means that there is a greater diversity of participatory experiences today, and these might interest or accommodate a greater range of people. Such an outcome seems especially likely for groups and causes on the political right, which rarely used protest tactics in the past. The findings of this study show that 65 percent of individuals have, at one point in their lives, engaged in an SMO or contentious political activity. This percentage is probably lower than the number of current high school seniors who will engage in such groups or activities over the course of their lives. Hence, today there is even more reason to accept the overall assertion that social movement participation is the purview of the many and not just an isolated few. Therefore, social movements and contentious political activity must be understood as part of the lives of ordinary people and not just a few highly committed "activists." Such an understanding of social movements and protest suggests a more engaged model of democracy in the contemporary period, with the actions of many individuals promoting social change.

We would also expect that the transfer and abeyance trajectories of participation would be even more common for today's high school seniors than they have been for previous cohorts. The growth and diversification of issues, tactics, and groups creates new opportunities for a variety of people to engage in contentious politics. Individuals who are politically on the left or the right, who are more or less interested in engaging in risky or costly activity, and who have varying levels of commitment to social issues now have many more opportunities to engage in civil society and to join social movements. Consequently, not only should more people be expected to participate but once involved they should also be more likely to follow a trajectory of transfer or abeyance over time. Permanent disengagement seems less likely for the current generation because opportunities for involvement are readily available and the costs and risks of engaging are relatively low.

Finally, if this study were conducted with the current cohort of high school seniors, it would also likely show a slightly different profile of engagement. Since Putnam's (2000) influential work, there has been a great deal of discussion of a large-scale process of disengagement from civil society in the United States. Today, as the argument goes, instead of participating in bowling leagues and community groups, we bowl alone and often stay at home. While this thesis has been criticized on many fronts, there is broad-based evidence that the character of civic engagement may be changing. Earlier cohorts, particularly the sample from the 1960s and 1970s examined in this study, were engaged in a civil society that emphasized the importance of formal organizations and participation within such organizations. Over time, however, engagement in organized activity may paradoxically be declining at the same time as participation in protest is rising. In fact, since 1982 even the cohort in the survey component of this study saw declining involvement in groups, from a high of 28.3 percent in 1982 to only 9.2 percent in 1997. In contrast, engagement in protest activity has increased slowly and steadily throughout the period from 1965 (15.2%) to 1997 (21.7%). These changes may reflect a larger shift in civil society away from involvement in groups. In addition, the growth of self-expressive values encourages participation in activities that are less constrained, more assertive, and more direct (Dalton 2008). With this in mind, we would expect that a repeat of this study using a later cohort of individuals would likely show lower levels of group membership but higher levels of engagement in protest activities.

The expectation that there will be higher levels and more varied forms of engagement among future cohorts of social movement participants reemphasizes the central tenets of this book. First, involvement in social movements and contentious political activity is something that a large number of people experience, and over time such involvement has become even more prevalent. In addition, the majority of individuals who participate in these groups and activities engage episodically or disengage over time. This widespread participation and the diversity of modes of engagement show the richness and vitality of civil society. Examining what happens after the protest, once the signs are put away and the television cameras are gone, sheds light on the various ways in which individual citizens interact with civil society. Through this lens, we can see how many citizens, from the passionately committed to the episodically engaged, can create social change.

Reference Matter

Appendix: Methodology

This book relies on the analysis of two distinct data sets. Chapters 2 and 3 present analyses of quantitative panel data collected by M. Kent Jennings and colleagues (1983, 1991, 2004, 2005, 2007). Chapters 4, 5, and 6 are based on qualitative interviews of individuals who were, at one time, members of one of four social movement organizations: a Catholic Worker community, the United Farm Workers, Concerned Women for America, and the (pseudonymous) Homeowners Association.

Quantitative Data

Data Source

M. Kent Jennings and colleagues (1983, 1991, 2004, 2005, 2007) have assembled data on political participation over the life course. These data sets are available through the Inter-university Consortium for Political and Social Research through the following catalogue numbers: ICPSR07286-v3 (1965),[1] ICPSR07779 (1973),[2] ICPSR09553 (1982),[3] and ICPSR04023-v2 (1997).[4] I gratefully acknowledge Jennings and his colleagues for their willingness to make these unique data sets available to the academic community and public. These data allow me to assess the predictors of whether or not an individual participates in contentious politics as well as the trajectory of her engagement over time (see Table A1 for the trajectory coding).

Sampling Procedures

These data sets are derived from a longitudinal national probability sample of high school seniors. These seniors were initially interviewed in 1965 ($N =$

Table A1 Coding of participation trajectory

Trajectory	Time 1	Time 2	Time 3	Time 4
Persistence	y	y	y	y
	—	y	y	y
	—	—	y	y
Abeyance	—	y	—	y
	y	y	—	y
	y	—	—	y
	y	—	y	—
	y	—	y	y
Disengagement	y	—	—	—
	y	y	—	—
	y	y	y	—
	—	y	—	—
	—	y	y	—
	—	—	y	—
Excluded	—	—	—	—
	—	—	—	y

NOTE: y = participated in a social movement organization or protest event in this time period.

— = did not participate in a social movement organization or protest event in this time period.

N.B. It is important to note that individuals could reengage in activism at a later time after the last survey in 1997 had been completed.

1669), with subsequent surveys of the same individuals conducted in 1973, 1982, and 1997 ($N = 934$, 56% of original sample). To achieve a national probability sample of 1965 high school seniors, a selection of American schools was first made with probability proportionate to size. About nine in ten of the schools selected agreed to take part in the study. Within schools, systematic random samples were taken. In total, 1,669 students were interviewed in 1965, an average of 17 seniors per school. And of those seniors selected, the response rate was over 99 percent. As a result of this sampling procedure, the youth panel is a probability sample of the American high school senior class of 1965. (For information on the sampling procedures and how the 1973 sample were found and interviewed, see Jennings and Niemi [1981], appendix A.)

It is important to note that some subjects were lost from the sample over time for a variety of reasons. Nevertheless, Jennings (2002, appendix) posits that panel bias over the course of the project appears to be slight. Comparisons between those who remained in the panel over the four waves and those who dropped out of the study on politically relevant variables drawn from the 1965 interviews reveal that the panelists were slightly more engaged in and knowledgeable about politics and had slightly more liberal attitudes. In no case, however, did panel status account for more than 2 percent of the variance in these scores.

Qualitative Sample

Case Selection

The interviews presented in Chapters 4, 5, and 6 of this book are derived from a sample of individuals in four social movement organizations. These organizations were chosen through dimensional sampling (Arnold 1970; see also Johnson 1990). This sampling procedure involves three steps. First, one must explicitly delineate the universe to which one eventually seeks to generalize. Second, one must specify the most important dimensions along which the members of this universe vary and develop a typology that includes the various combinations of values of these dimensions. Finally, this typology is used as a sampling frame for selecting a small number of cases from the universe, typically drawing one case from each cell in the typology. Dimensional sampling is based on a theoretical framework but not on preconceived theory. In light of this, I have selected a dimensional sample of four SMOs (social movement organizations) that vary along two dimensions: issue scope and level of hierarchy. In this way, I am able to assess the effect of these two organizational variables on participants' trajectory of participation over time.

I examine issue scope by comparing multi-issue and single-issue groups. Multi-issue groups are groups that work on at least two issues that they see as connected to a larger, overarching ideology. Single-issue groups work on one specific cause and do not explicitly tie this cause to other issues. I also assess the role of hierarchy and compare groups that are very hierarchical with those that are more egalitarian. I selected groups that represent the four possible combinations of these two variables in order to examine the roles of these organizational factors in leading individuals to follow certain trajectories of participation over time. In addition, I chose movement organizations that represent different issue areas and ideological perspectives. I included groups on the political left and right, religious and nonreligious groups, large national groups and local grassroots groups, and a labor group and a neighborhood group. Literatures on these different types of groups and issues are not often in dialogue, and this book begins to address this hiatus.

In each of the groups, I selected 15 participants who were active in either 1970/71 (for the United Farm Workers and Catholic Workers) or 1980/81 (for Concerned Women for America and the Homeowners Association).[5] I interviewed these individuals and traced their participation over time, from their initial foray into contentious politics to the present day. This research design allows me to compare individuals who remained active over time with those who disengaged, transferred, or followed an abeyance trajectory. As demonstrated in Table 5, the demographic profile of this group is similar in age and background to the quantitative panel sample examined in Chapters 2 and 3 and the national population of the United States in this period.

Selection of Interview Samples

In the Catholic Worker community, I began by locating a primary contact, who assisted me in contacting other past participants. Because of the relatively small size of this social movement community, I was able to interview 15 of the 16 individuals who were actively involved in the community in 1970. As a result, my sample is virtually identical to the population of individuals in this group at that time. I chose this time frame because it was just after the initial group had moved into the communal house in the city, enabling me to contact the founding participants as well as the early new recruits to the community. For demographic information on the sample, see Table 5.

I had two methods for contacting past participants in Concerned Women for America. Initially I called the head office of CWA and asked if they would release the names of women who had previously participated in the group. They were reluctant to share membership lists but agreed to put me in touch with a woman who still worked at CWA who had initially gotten involved in the early 1980s. I selected this time period because it was one year after the founding of the group and there was already a large membership, but it was before the group moved to Washington, DC, and consequently there was a focus on local work at the time. I snowball-sampled from this woman to four others but found that all five of these women had similar stories of increased participation over time culminating in leading state chapters of the organization. As this was but one trajectory, I sought to find other women with a variety of experiences. I did this by reading issues of the group's newsletter from 1980 to 1982. These newsletters listed new prayer action chapter leaders throughout the country with their phone numbers.[6] I randomly selected ten of these women and contacted them through Internet White Pages searches. All ten of the women I contacted agreed to be interviewed.

While the United Farm Workers and its supporters encompass individuals across the United States and outside the country, from college campuses
to union halls to consumers at the supermarket who refused to buy certain
products, my analysis is based on an examination of UFW volunteers who
lived for a time at La Paz, the union headquarters, in the early 1970s. I selected
this time period because it was just after the union headquarters moved to La
Paz and there was already a large community living there. I narrowed the
population to La Paz residents for three main reasons. First, moving to La Paz
indicates a comparable level of commitment to the movement; this is prefer-
able to comparing individuals who moved to La Paz with those who simply
supported the union by refusing to purchase grapes during the boycott. Second, while at La Paz, the participants shared a common living and working
experience. Finally, La Paz bounds my population frame and makes it possible to select in an intentional fashion. While it is not possible to select randomly, as there is no list of residents at La Paz, I snowball-sampled 15 individuals who lived there in the early 1970s from the total residency of La Paz at the
time, which was approximately 175 to 200 people.[7]

Finally, I selected members of the Homeowners Association by contacting the board of directors, which is clearly listed on all group newsletters. The
board of directors of the HA, formed in 1981, consisted of 19 individuals; I was
able to contact and interview 15 of these individuals for this study. Of the remaining four individuals on the board, I was unable to contact one, two had
passed away, and one was ill and declined to participate in the study.

Interview Schedule

The interviews lasted from 45 minutes to four hours and were tape-recorded
and transcribed in their entirety. The interview consisted of seven sections
(for a full interview schedule, see Table A2). I began by asking questions about
the focal movements (CW, CWA, HA, and UFW), asking about the core concerns of the group, the organization of the group, the influence of individuals
in the group, the goals of the group, and how effective they thought the group
was at achieving its goals. The second section of the interview concerned initial engagement in the group, starting with when, how, and why they initially
joined. I also asked about their lives at that time (their jobs, education, age,
and location). In addition, I asked if they were involved in other groups at the
time when they initially engaged.

The third section of the interview examined participation in the focal
group over time. I asked respondents how long they were involved in the

Table A2 Schedule of interview questions

1. The movement

   Can you tell me a bit about [social movement]?

   a. What were the core concerns of this group?

   b. How was the group organized? (Were there leaders? Was it formal/informal? Hierarchical or egalitarian?)

   c. What were the goals of the group?

   d. How effective do you think this group was at achieving its goals?

   e. How much input or influence did individual members have in the group?

2. Initial involvement

   a. When did you initially join this group? How old were you?

   b. How did you initially get involved in this movement? Were you actively recruited?

   c. Why did you initially join this group?

   d. Did you know people in the movement when you first got involved?

   e. Were you in other social movement groups before this one or at the time you initially got involved?

3. Sustained participation

   a. How long were you involved in this movement?

   b. What was going on in your life in general when you were participating in this movement? (school, family, work, etc.)

   c. What sorts of activities did you engage in with this movement?

   d. How much time did you spend participating in this movement?

   e. What sorts of relationships did you have with people in the movement? (How close/personal, how many people were you friends with?)

   f. How important was this movement to you and the way you saw yourself?

   g. Did your participation in the movement change over time?

4. Disengagement

   Are you still involved in this movement?

   a. If so, has your participation changed over time?

      i. Do you spend more or less time working on movement activities?

      ii. Do you still engage in the same type of activities?

      iii. Do you have more or fewer ties to other movement members?

      iv. Is this movement more or less important to you than it was in the past?

      v. Why do you continue to participate in this movement?

   b. If not, do you remember how and why you stopped participating in this movement?

      i. What was going on in your life in general when you stopped participating in this movement? (career/school, family, etc.)

      ii. Why did you stop participating in this group?

      iii. How did you feel about the way the group was structured or run?

      iv. Did you stop participating suddenly or slowly over time?

      v. Do you still sympathize with the goals of the movement?

      vi. Do you still think of yourself as someone who supports that cause?

Table A2 (*continued*)

---

     vii. Has the way you think about yourself changed since you stopped participating in this movement? If so, how?

    viii. Are you still in contact with the people you knew in the movement?

5. Later participation

   Since you stopped participating in that group, have you been involved in any other groups? Or, if you are still involved in the group, do you also participate in other groups?

  a. If no, why not?

  b. If yes, what other groups have you been a member of?

   Can you tell me a bit about that group?

     i. When did you begin participating in that group?

    ii. How long did you participate in that group?

    iii. What sorts of activities did you engage in with that group?

    iv. How much time did you spend participating in that group?

     v. What sorts of relationships did you have with the people in that group? (close/personal? How many were you friends with?)

   Repeat questions i–v for all groups of which the individual was or is a member.

6. Other political participation

  a. What other sorts of political activities have you engaged in?

   Voting? Volunteering in political organizations? Signing petitions? Boycotting a product? Letters to officials? Protesting? Striking (or respecting picket lines)? Other activities?

7. Sociodemographic variables

  a. Age

  b. Gender

  c. Religion

  d. Religiosity

  e. Education

  f. Ethnicity

  g. Marital status

  h. Children

  i. Occupation (over time)

  j. Political identification

---

group, in what sorts of activities they engaged, how much time they spent with the group, the types and number of relationships they had with other participants in the group, and how important this group was to them and the way they saw themselves. Finally, I asked if their participation in the group changed over time in terms of time spent, activities, and relationships with other participants.

The fourth section focused on disengagement from the focal group, if that occurred. I asked if they were still involved in the group and, if so, how their

Table A3 Interview sample information

Group and number	Pseudonym	Gender	Age	Occupation	Years in focal group	Trajectory
Catholic Workers						
1	Brenda	Female	66	Nun	4	Transfer
2	Patricia	Female	55	Lab technician	14	Transfer
3	Phil	Male	55	Social worker	4	Abeyance
4	Nancy	Female	70	Nurse	36	Persist
5	Daniel	Male	67	Priest	22	Transfer
6	Jeremy	Male	62	Shop owner	14	Disengage
7	Arnold	Male	57	Librarian	3	Abeyance
8	Janet	Female	68	ESL teacher	20	Transfer
9	Sean	Male	81	Judge	15	Disengage
10	Margaret	Female	63	Nurse	16	Abeyance
11	John	Male	53	Carpenter	2	Disengage
12	Dennis	Male	68	Social worker	2	Transfer
13	Chris	Male	53	Social worker	15	Transfer
14	Harriet	Female	57	Editor	5	Abeyance
15	Neal	Male	53	Nonprofit	10	Transfer
Concerned Women for America						
1	Joanne	Female	57	Stay at home	23	Persist
2	Christine	Female	55	Consultant	20	Persist
3	Sally	Female	51	Stay at home	20	Persist
4	Penny	Female	63	Stay at home	18	Persist
5	Judy	Female	51	Stay at home	10	Transfer
6	Helen	Female	80	Social work	1	Disengage
7	Rebecca	Female	68	Stay at home	6 mo.	Disengage
8	Shirley	Female	50	Stay at home	3 mo.	Disengage
9	Betty	Female	61	Teacher	2	Disengage
10	Lisa	Female	76	Stay at home	6 mo.	Disengage
11	Ellen	Female	62	Teacher	6 mo.	Disengage
12	Irene	Female	81	Manager	1	Disengage
13	Connie	Female	70	Stay at home	2	Disengage
14	Ann	Female	65	Stay at home	3	Disengage
15	Virginia	Female	60	Stay at home	1	Disengage

Group and number	Pseudonym	Gender	Age	Occupation	Years in focal group	Trajectory
United Farm Workers						
1	Joan	Female	73	Farm worker	30	Persist
2	David	Male	56	Media consultant	26	Persist
3	Anthony	Male	59	Union organizer	15	Abeyance
4	Tom	Male	63	Lawyer	12	Disengage
5	Charlie	Male	72	Nonprofit	41	Persist
6	Andrew	Male	58	Consultant	5	Disengage
7	Valerie	Female	64	Social worker	5	Disengage
8	Kevin	Male	61	Union organizer	31	Persist
9	Karen	Female	52	Social worker	15	Abeyance
10	Cynthia	Female	57	Lawyer	22	Transfer
11	Mark	Male	53	Lawyer	7	Abeyance
12	Teresa	Female	48	At UFW	30	Persist
13	Bert	Male	70	Priest	12	Transfer
14	James	Male	65	Education	12	Transfer
15	Sylvia	Female	64	Real estate	12	Transfer
Homeowners Association						
1	Amy	Female	59	Stay at home	16	Transfer
2	Diana	Female	70	Manager	5	Disengage
3	Polly	Female	69	Manager	13	Disengage
4	Robert	Male	62	Lawyer	5	Disengage
5	Jimmy	Male	65	Doctor	6	Disengage
6	Lynn	Female	51	Stay at home	6	Transfer
7	Peggy	Female	75	Stay at home	3	Disengage
8	Vicki	Female	71	Entrepreneur	4	Disengage
9	Sherry	Female	77	Stay at home	8	Disengage
10	Charlotte	Female	55	Teacher	10	Disengage
11	Ruth	Female	61	Lawyer	4	Abeyance
12	Anna	Female	46	Teacher	7	Disengage
13	Darlene	Female	80	Sales	3	Disengage
14	Henry	Male	75	Architect	20	Transfer
15	Kenneth	Male	47	Engineer	3	Disengage

participation had or had not changed over time. In particular, I asked if their participation had changed in terms of time spent, the nature of their ties with other members, the importance of the group to the way they see themselves, and the types of activities in which they engaged.

I also queried later participation. Whether or not they continued to participate in the focal group, I asked if they were currently involved in other groups and, if so, the amount of time, activities, and the types of relationships they had with the people in any additional groups in which they participated. I repeated these questions for every additional group in which they participated. I also asked about other types of political participation such as voting, volunteering in political organizations, signing petitions, boycotting products, writing letters to officials, protesting, and striking or respecting picket lines.

I concluded with some sociodemographic questions concerning age, gender, religion, religiosity (in terms of attendance), education, ethnicity, marital status, children, occupation (over time), and political party identification. These questions were put at the end of the interview because they can be seen as personal and it is advisable to ask them after rapport is achieved. Finally, I asked why they continued to participate in their group over time, moved to another group or groups, or stopped participating in social movements. I also asked why they thought other people leave social movements over time.

Biographical reconstruction and memory failure are always problems in retrospective interviewing. A number of techniques were employed to protect against these biases. To address the accuracy of recall, I structured my questions around past events rather than past attitudes because memories of events are more reliable (Markus 1986; Schacter 1996). In addition, research shows that more salient, less repetitive events are remembered with particular accuracy (Beckett et al. 2000; Scott and Alwin 1998, 114). To this end, I asked respondents about memorable life events, such as marriage or the birth of a child, and then asked if this event had occurred before or after pivotal participation events. This made it possible to assess more clearly the temporal order of events. For descriptive information on the qualitative interview sample, see Table A3.

Notes

Chapter 1

1. Contentious politics here refers to "collective activity on the part of claimants ... relying at least in part on noninstitutional forms of interaction with elites, opponents, or the state" (Tarrow 1996, 874). Social movement organizations can and do engage in this type of activity, but contentious political activity can also occur without being coordinated by a social movement organization. I examine both engagement in social movement organizations and participation in activities of protest that are not affiliated with social movement groups. I characterize contentious political activity as the combination of engagement in social movement organizations and in activities of protest, including marches, demonstrations, and rallies. I chose not to define the activities and groups in this analysis more broadly as civic participation because this would then include other activities such as voting, participating in political parties, and participating in nonpolitical groups, such as churches and sports clubs. While these kinds of groups are important parts of civil society and foster social trust among citizens, they are qualitatively different from contentious political activity.

2. The two most prominent leaders of the United Farm Workers, Cesar Chavez and Dolores Huerta, have a total of 641 books written by and about them, while there are only 111 books written about the United Farm Workers. Dorothy Day and Peter Maurin, another major leader of the Catholic Worker movement, have 348 books written by and about them, while the Catholic Worker movement is the subject of only 264 books. These numbers are based on an Internet search of books with these names on Amazon.com.

3. The biographies of Karen and Amy (both pseudonyms) are derived from interviews I conducted with 60 individuals who participated in four social movement organizations: the United Farm Workers, a Catholic Worker community, Concerned Women for America, and a homeowners association. These interviews form the basis

of my analyses in Chapters 4, 5, and 6. For more information on the history of these groups, the sampling procedures, and the interview questions, see Chapter 4.

4. The concept of abeyance at the organizational level was introduced by Verta Taylor (1989). I extend this concept by applying it to individual participation trajectories over time. This concept will be discussed in more detail later in this chapter.

5. This model is illustrated in Figure 1. It will be discussed in more detail later in this chapter.

6. There has been some work by Bert Klandermans (1997) and Pamela Oliver (1984) that examines movement organizations with varying degrees of risk and cost. In general, however, the literature on participation over time has focused on movements and organizations that are high cost and high risk.

7. For example, Fendrich (1993), Jennings (1987), and McAdam (1989) conducted follow-up studies of past activists.

8. The studies by Bird and Reimer (1982), Passy and Giugni (2000), Sandell (1999), Veen and Klandermans (1989), and Weiss (1963) are exceptions. Each of these is a case study that examines one social movement organization over time. None of the studies, however, compare groups, examine the role of group context, or follow individual participants over time. These studies will be discussed in more detail in Chapter 3.

9. In Downton and Wehr's (1997) study of peace movement activists, they refer to moving from one peace organization to another, which is transfer within one movement, as shifting.

10. Staggenborg (1987) also discusses the related concept of "organizational interaction sites." These sites promote the development of shared meanings about social issues among persons with similar life-style preferences both before and after contact with the movement. She argues that continued commitment is likely if the lifestyle preferences of the individual continue to bring him or her into contact with the movement. For example, attendance at church can increase the likelihood that individuals who are already sympathetic to the pro-life cause will be recruited by activists they meet through this religious engagement.

11. Taylor's original conceptualization of movement abeyance structures focuses on abeyance as a holding pattern of an organization, and in her work she posits that movement culture was one of the major elements that helped to maintain these movement abeyance structures over time (1989). For individuals, these structures include social ties, tactics, and ideological commitments, which also have a cultural component.

12. This theoretical model is elaborated throughout the course of this book. More detailed discussions of research and theory concerning each of the relationships in this model are provided in later empirical chapters.

13. For more information about this data set, including sampling procedures, see

the Appendix. For information on specific variables used and question wording, see Chapter 2.

14. See Polletta and Jasper (2001).

15. For more information on the history of each of these groups, see Chapter 4. For information on the sampling techniques used in each group, see the Appendix.

16. Biographical reconstruction and memory failure are always problems in retrospective interviewing. A number of techniques were employed to guard against these biases and are discussed in detail in the Appendix.

17. For more information on the qualitative sample and a comparison with the national population of the United States at the time, see Table 5 and the Appendix.

18. There are many homeowner groups in Santa Monica. The name "Homeowners Association" was chosen to protect the anonymity of the individuals interviewed in this study.

19. There were many autobiographies written by members of the United Farm Workers, in particular. There were also a number of books written about Catholic Worker communities (although not the specific community I study in this project). These biographies and autobiographies were written both by leaders and by rank-and-file members.

20. The transfer trajectory cannot be assessed with these data. The specific name of the group in which an individual participated is not listed, and therefore an individual who is active in different groups in all four periods and an individual who is active in the same group in all four periods appear to be identical.

Chapter 2

1. The information on these four individuals is based on the interviews conducted for the second half of this book. For more information on the history of these groups, the sampling procedures, and the interview questions, see Chapter 4.

2. Social ties are another significant predictor of engagement in social movements and collective action. There is an extensive body of work that finds that social ties lead to initial engagement and could help individuals remain active within groups or campaigns over time (for a discussion of the literature on the role of social ties, see Chapter 5). The Jennings survey instrument, on which the analyses in this chapter are based, did not include questions about social ties. Consequently, the role of social ties cannot be assessed in the quantitative analyses presented in this book. In addition, the important role of the organizational and relational context of participation cannot be assessed with the survey instrument. In order to address these limitations, I have presented extensive qualitative data on the role of social ties and interaction in social movement engagement in Chapter 5.

3. Efficacy is both an ideology and a social psychological resource. I categorize it as an ideology here because I see it as a belief that individuals have the ability to shape

the world around them. The classification of efficacy either as an ideology or as a so-cial psychological resource does not fundamentally affect my overall findings or the theoretical implications of these findings as presented in this chapter.

4. The Civic Voluntarism Model proposed by Verba and colleagues (1995) high-lights the role of a broad range of psychological, institutional, and material resources available to an individual that predict political participation. These include tradi-tional resources such as time and money, psychological characteristics (such as politi-cal efficacy), and civic skills (such as language skills) (Verba et al. 1995). The analyses presented in this book assess a selection of these variables, including the resource of time (as it relates to biographical availability), psychological characteristics (such as ideology and efficacy), and civic skills (such as knowledge).

5. The biographical availability perspective does not simply imply that those without obligations will be more likely to engage in activism. It also notes that move-ment participation is shaped by changing life circumstances. Also, certain life-course statuses might be correlated with distinct forms of movement activism. For example, full-time employment is related to labor activism, and parenthood is correlated with engaging in education or other issues related to children.

6. The negotiated management style of policing (McPhail et al. 1998), which in-volves coordination with and respect for protesters, is the general philosophy em-ployed by police departments in recent years. Nevertheless, there are still episodes of police violence, intimidation, and aggression. In addition, many protest campaigns of the past experienced high levels of repression and violence on the part of the police and the army.

7. It is important to note that individuals who are employed are more likely to be union members. And, as union membership is associated with increased social move-ment activity, this may partly account for the higher levels of participation among the employed.

8. There has also been work examining the participation of Asian Americans (Okamoto 2003; Wong 2005; Xu 2005), Latinas/os (Martinez 2005, 2008), and Muslim Americans (Bakalian and Bozorgmehr 2005). However, because of the small number of individuals who did not identify as either white or African American in the Jen-nings and Stoker panel data, I was unable to separately assess the participation of these other groups.

9. The survey also asked about membership in seven other types of nonpoliti-cal groups: church, fraternal, neighborhood, sport, informal, professional, and ethnic groups. The explicitly political wording in the questions about civic and community groups provides confidence that they are the only ones tapping contentious group activity; further analysis confirms this by showing an overlap between membership in the civic and community groups and contentious acts (protesting, marching, ral-lying, and demonstrating). That is, individuals who belonged to a civic or commu-nity group were very likely to have engaged in contentious political activities and vice

versa. Belonging to the other groups, however, did not correlate strongly with contentious political activity.

10. This is admittedly a broader definition of contentious political activity than is typical for those who associate such activity primarily with the major social and political movements over the last century. Yet contentious politics is in fact broader and more widespread than these well-known movements. According to Tarrow (1996), contentious politics is "collective activity on the part of claimants relying at least in part on non-institutional forms of interaction with elites, opponents, or the state" (874). From this perspective, contentious activity is simply noninstitutional and works outside of the regular routes of power (elections, political parties, etc.). This does include major national or international movements, but it also includes civic and community groups that interact with local elites and mobilize for collective goods or policies.

11. The questions are as follows: "About how many years does a U.S. senator serve?"; "Marshal Tito is a leader in what country?"; "Do you happen to know about how many members there are on the U.S. Supreme Court?"; "Who is the governor of (name of this state) now?"; "During World War II, which nation had a great number of concentration camps for Jews?"; and "Do you happen to remember whether President Franklin Delano Roosevelt was a Republican or Democrat? (If necessary): Which?"

12. Respondents were asked, "Generally speaking, do you usually think of yourself as a Republican, a Democrat, an independent, or what?" If they responded that they thought of themselves as a Republican or a Democrat, they were asked, "Would you call yourself a strong (R) (D) or a not very strong (R) (D)?" If they responded that they were independent, they were asked, "Do you think of yourself as closer to the Republican or Democratic Party?"

13. Alternatively, religiosity could be operationalized as an individual's level of devoutness or commitment to his or her religion. These alternative measures were not included in this data set. Therefore, frequency of attendance was chosen because it is a behavioral measure of religiosity.

14. In the 1965 survey, the questions were worded as "people like my family."

15. Respondents were not asked about living with a same-sex spouse until the last survey. For this reason, I could not include this response category.

16. Respondents were asked to list all the people in their household. Son, daughter, stepson, stepdaughter, grandson, and granddaughter were considered children in the home.

17. I used the multiple imputation (MI) method to deal with missing data rather than other strategies such as listwise or pairwise deletion because this strategy assumes only that data are missing at random (MAR), in contrast to listwise deletion, which requires the stronger assumption that the data are missing completely at random (MCAR) (Allison 2002; Rubin 1987).

18. Clearly individuals are shaped by their historical period. However, because

respondent age and year are perfectly correlated in these data, as all individuals in the study were 18 in 1965, it is not possible to examine the effect of historical period separate from analyses of age and aging processes. Future work examining individuals of varying ages over the life course could enrich our understanding of the effect of historical period by separating the effects of age and aging from the impact of larger historical processes.

Chapter 3

1. The biographies are derived from a sample of 60 individuals who participated in four social movement organizations: the United Farm Workers, a Catholic Worker community, Concerned Women for America, and a homeowners association. For more information on the history of these groups, see Chapter 4. For information on the sampling procedures and interview questions, see the Appendix.

2. It is important to note that the surveys are not equidistant and do not cover the same number of years. The 1965 survey was conducted when the respondents were 18 years old. They thus had had a very limited number of years to engage in politics and were, as a consequence, mostly asked about engagement in school politics such as student government. The subsequent three periods were 7, 8, and 14 years long, respectively. Obviously, the fact that the final period was twice as long as the two preceding it allowed the respondents to have had more time to have participated in advance of the final survey. This could result in an increase in the raw number of people who had participated in the final period and would be problematic if the analysis were predicting the number of times individuals engaged in contentious activity. But this limitation should not affect the overall correlates of participation.

3. The data presented in the trajectory models are right censored, which means that the event of interest is to the right of our data point. In other words, if the individuals were surveyed again, they might have joined or left a group at some time after the last data point (to the right on the time scale). In essence, we do not know what happens to individuals after the last survey period; while some individuals who were disengaged during the last period will remain so, others might reengage in a social movement later. This is an important theoretical consideration but cannot be addressed with the data presented in this analysis.

Chapter 4

1. For a discussion of this limitation of the survey data, see Chapter 1.

2. Gamson (1990) delineates three features that characterize bureaucratic organizations, which are groups that are hierarchical, centralized, and formalized. First, such groups possess a written document that states the purpose of the organization and its provision for operation. Second, the group maintains a formal list of members. Finally, the group possesses three or more levels of internal division.

3. For more discussion of the role of social ties and interaction in social movement participation, see Chapter 5.

4. These holistic ideologies are similar to what Snow and Benford (1992) and Kubal (1998) refer to as master frames. Master frames are general interpretive packages. They perform the same functions as movement-specific collective action frames but on a larger scale. While a collective action frame is an "interpretive schemata that simplifies and condenses the 'world out there' by selectively punctuating and encoding objects, situations, events, experiences, and sequences of actions" (Snow and Benford 1992, 137), master frames do the same thing but may be applied to any number of movement organizations. Thus the larger, holistic ideologies that multi-issue groups often subscribe to are similar to master frames.

5. Female, 68, ESL teacher.

6. Male, 55, social worker.

7. Male, 53, nonprofit worker.

8. Romantic partnering both enabled the persistent participation of individual members (because individuals with partners in the group were more likely to remain) and precipitated the disengagement of individuals after the breakup of a relationship. When a romantic relationship ended, one partner often left the group.

9. Other major Christian Right organizations founded in this period are the National Christian Action Coalition, the Religious Roundtable, the Christian Voice, the Moral Majority, the Freedom Council, and the American Coalition for Traditional Values (Moen 1992).

10. The group moved to Washington in order to have a larger impact on national government policy.

11. According to CWA newsletters from 1981: 3(5), p. 2; 4(2), p. 3.

12. There were only two exceptions to this: two women heard about CWA from family members and wrote to the organization to get information; at that time, they were asked to be prayer action chapter leaders in their area.

13. There are many homeowners groups in Santa Monica. The name "Homeowners Association" was chosen to protect the anonymity of the individuals interviewed in this study.

14. Male, 74, architect; female, 77, stay-at-home.

15. CST is a pseudonym given to this incarnation of the group to protect the group's anonymity.

16. CPSI is a pseudonym given to this initiative to protect the group's anonymity.

17. The board, once formed, was not technically exclusive; other members could, in theory, join the board even if they had not attended this first meeting. In reality, however, the board did not add any additional members for the first two years.

18. By definition, the term *profession* refers to occupations that include the following: some central regulatory body to ensure the standard of performance of in-

dividual members; a code of conduct; careful management of knowledge in relation to the expertise that constitutes the basis of the profession's activities; and control of numbers, selection, and training of new entrants (Marshall 1998). Examples of professions include jobs with varying levels of status, such as doctors, lawyers, social workers, and teachers.

Chapter 5

1. Two individuals in CWA and one individual in the HA sought out the group without being recruited by either leaders or rank-and-file members of the group.

2. Fisher's exact test (similar to the chi-square test but controlling for the small number of observations) shows that the difference in the cells is significant at the 0.001 level.

3. Fisher's exact test is significant at the 0.01 level.

4. In this analysis, both the CW and the HA are categorized as egalitarian groups. However, it is quite possible that the concept of egalitarianism is differently understood among members of the CW and the HA because of the groups' different ideologies. Recent work by authors such as Hallett and Ventresca (2006) argues that institutions are "inhabited" and that we must understand the actions, interactions, and meanings that occur within organizations accordingly. These authors offer an "inhabited institutions approach," arguing that institutions provide the raw materials and guidelines for social interactions while being constructed by these interactions. In this analysis, I categorize the CW and the HA as egalitarian groups because they do not have formal leaders, a clear division of labor, or a defined chain of command, and I argue that these features have real consequences for the participation of members over time. At the same time, however, I recognize that the reasons for this organizational structure and how this structure is understood by group members may differ between the two groups.

5. The name of the festival has been changed to protect the anonymity of the group.

6. Fisher's exact test is significant at the 0.001 level.

Chapter 6

1. Individuals engaging in social movement activities may choose not to identify as activists for many reasons. For example, Bobel (2007) highlights how individuals engaging in social movement activities may not identify as activists because they see activists as "perfect standards" of politics who must "live the issue" and demonstrate relentless dedication in order to merit the label. With this definition in mind, many individuals may not apply the label of activist to themselves because they feel they cannot live up to the extreme standard.

2. Not only are the specific goals of the groups leftist in nature (reducing inequality resulting from structural social arrangements, and antiwar and pacifist causes)

but also all the group members whom I interviewed self-identified as either Democrats or Green Party supporters.

3. Because CWA and the HA did not consider themselves to be SMOs, it was insufficient simply to ask about past social movement engagement. Interviewees were therefore asked if they had had earlier participatory experiences in a wider variety of groups, including community groups, public policy groups, and civic organizations.

4. Religious organizations can be SMOs if they engage in activities aimed at changing society as a whole. For example, many conservative Protestant churches mobilize to restrict abortion rights and participate in protests and other social movement tactics to achieve this goal. The former CWA women I interviewed, however, did not participate in their churches in these ways. They were engaged in Bible study groups, social committees, and other internal activities not aimed at challenging larger social systems.

5. Focusing on a narrower set of issues is not meant to imply lower levels of commitment to the group or the beliefs of the group. It is meant to indicate a more bounded set of concerns that are not explicitly tied to other social issues outside the group's main focus by the leadership.

6. There is a stereotype that most or all UFW participants are themselves farm workers. If this were true, it would not be surprising that there were few people who transferred to other causes over time. However, the UFW is a much more varied group than this stereotype would suggest (see Chapter 4 for a history and description of this group). The UFW is ethnically diverse, and many members of the UFW are, in fact, from the middle or upper-middle class. These individuals often initially engaged in the UFW while at university or through religious organizations. This makes the low levels of transfer even more surprising, as these individuals do not necessarily have a personal connection to farm worker issues because of their biographies.

Chapter 7

1. These UFW members were not members of the specific CW community studied in this analysis; they were members of other, similar communities in other cities.

Appendix

1. M. Kent Jennings. 2007. Student–Parent Socialization Study, 1965 [Computer file]. Conducted by M. Kent Jennings, University of California. ICPSR07286-v3. Ann Arbor, MI: Inter-university Consortium for Political and Social Research [producer and distributor]. doi:10.3886/ICPSR07286.

2. M. Kent Jennings and Richard G. Niemi. 1991. Youth–Parent Socialization Panel Study, 1965–1973 [Computer file]. Conducted by University of Michigan, Center for Political Studies. 2nd ICPSR ed. Ann Arbor, MI: Inter-university Consortium for Political and Social Research [producer and distributor]. doi:10.3886/ICPSR07779.

3. M. Kent Jennings, Gregory B. Markus, and Richard G. Niemi. 1991. Youth–

Parent Socialization Panel Study, 1965–1982: Three Waves Combined [Computer file]. Ann Arbor, MI: University of Michigan, Center for Political Studies/Survey Research Center [producers], 1983. Ann Arbor, MI: Inter-university Consortium for Political and Social Research [distributor]. doi:10.3886/ICPSR09553.

4. M. Kent Jennings and Laura Stoker. 2005. Youth–Parent Socialization Panel Study, 1965–1997: Youth Wave IV, 1997 [Computer file]. ICPSR04023-v2. Ann Arbor, MI: University of Michigan, Center for Political Studies/Survey Research Center [producer], 1997. Ann Arbor, MI: Inter-university Consortium for Political and Social Research [distributor]. doi:10.3886/ICPSR04023.

5. For more information on the history of each of these groups, see Chapter 4.

6. Being a prayer action chapter leader is not an indication of leadership in the way usually characterized in social movement scholarship. The women who were listed as prayer action chapter leaders, without exception, had not participated in the group at all before being listed as leaders and many of them did not even realize that they were listed as such in the newsletter. Anyone who showed interest in the organization from an area that did not have a prayer action chapter was listed as a prayer action chapter leader in her area in the newsletter.

7. Male, 70, priest.

References

Ahlbrandt, Roger S., Jr., and James V. Cunningham. 1979. *A New Public Policy for Neighborhood Preservation*. New York: Praeger.

Allison, Paul D. 2002. *Missing Data*. Thousand Oaks: Sage.

Arnold, D. O. 1970. "Dimensional Sampling: An Approach for Studying a Small Number of Cases." *American Sociologist* 5:147–50.

Babchuk, Nicholas, and Ralph V. Thompson. 1962. "The Voluntary Associations of Negroes." *American Sociological Review* 27:647–55.

Bakalian, Anny, and Mehdi Bozorgmehr. 2005. "Muslim American Mobilization." *Diaspora* 14(1): 7–43.

Barkan, Steven E., Steven F. Cohn, and William H. Whitaker. 1993. "Commitment across the Miles: Ideological and Microstructural Sources of Membership Support in a National Antihunger Organization." *Social Problems* 40:362–73.

Beckett, Megan, Maxine Weinstein, Noreen Goldman, and Lin Yu-Hsuan. 2000. "Do Health Interview Surveys Yield Reliable Data on Chronic Illness among Older Respondents?" *American Journal of Epidemiology* 151:315–23.

Bendyna, Mary E., John C. Green, Mark J. Rozell, and Clyde Wilcox. 2001. "Uneasy Alliance: Conservative Catholics and the Christian Right." *Sociology of Religion* 62(1): 51–64.

Beyerlein, Kraig, and John R. Hipp. 2006. "From Pews to Participation: The Effect of Congregation Activity and Context on Bridging Civic Engagement." *Social Problems* 53:97–117.

Bird, Frederick, and Bill Reimer. 1982. "Participation Rates in New Religious and Para-Religious Movements." *Journal for the Scientific Study of Religion* 21:1–14.

Blee, Kathleen M. 2002. *Inside Organized Racism: Women in the Hate Movement*. Berkeley: University of California Press.

Blumer, Herbert. 1969. *Symbolic Interactionism: Perspective and Method*. Englewood Cliffs, NJ: Prentice-Hall.

Bobel, C. 2007. "'I'm not an activist, though I've done a lot of it': Doing Activism, Being Activist and the 'Perfect Standard' in a Contemporary Movement." *Social Movement Studies* 6(2): 147–59.

Bradley, Graham. 2006. "Work Participation and Academic Performance: A Test of Alternative Propositions." *Journal of Education & Work* 19(5): 481–501.

Brady, Henry E., Kay Lehman Schlozman, and Sidney Verba. 1999. "Prospects for Participants: Rational Expectations and the Recruitment of Political Activists." *American Political Science Review* 93(1): 153–68.

Brownmiller, Susan. 1999. *In Our Time: Memoir of a Revolution*. New York: Dial Press.

Cable, Sherry. 1992. "Women's Social Movement Involvement: The Role of Structural Availability in Recruitment and Participation Processes." *Sociological Quarterly* 33:35–50.

Callero, Anthony J. 1985. "Role-Identity Salience." *Social Psychology Quarterly* 48:203–14.

Čapek, Stella M., and John Ingram Gilderbloom. 1992. *Community versus Commodity: Tenants and the American City*. Albany: State University of New York Press.

Clemens, Elisabeth S., and Martin D. Hughes. 2002. "Recovering Past Protest: Historical Research on Social Movements." In *Methods of Social Movement Research*, edited by Bert Klandermans and Suzanne Staggenborg, 201–30. Minneapolis: University of Minnesota Press.

Cohn, Steven F., Steven E. Barkan, and William A. Halteman. 2003. "Dimensions of Participation in a Professional Social-Movement Organization." *Sociological Inquiry* 73:311–37.

Connolly, Kate. 2004. "Maternal Activism on the Neighbourhood Level." *Journal of the Association for Research on Motherhood* 6(2):48–57.

Corrigall-Brown, Catherine, David A. Snow, Theron Quist, and Kelly Smith. 2009. "Protest among the Homeless: Explaining Differential Participation." *Sociological Perspectives* 52(3): 309–36.

Coy, Patrick. 2001. "An Experiment in Personalist Politics: The Catholic Worker Movement and Nonviolent Action." *Peace and Change* 26:78–94.

Cress, Daniel M., J. Miller McPherson, and Thomas Rotolo. 1997. "Competition and Commitment in Voluntary Memberships: The Paradox of Persistence and Participation." *Sociological Perspectives* 40:61–79.

Crozat, Matthew. 1998. "Are the Times A-Changin'? Assessing the Acceptance of Protest in Western Democracies." In *The Social Movement Society*, edited by David S. Meyer and Sidney Tarrow, 59–82. Oxford: Rowman and Littlefield.

Dalton, Russell J. 2008. *The Good Citizen: How a Younger Generation Is Reshaping American Politics*. Washington, DC: CQ Press.

Dalton, Russell J., Alix Van Sickle, and Steven Weldon. 2010. "The Individual-Institutional Nexus of Protest Behaviour." *British Journal of Political Science* 40(1): 51–73.

Diani, Mario. 2004. "Networks and Participation." In *The Blackwell Companion to Social Movements*, edited by David A. Snow, Sarah A. Soule, and H. Kreisi, 339–59. Malden, MA: Blackwell.

Downton, James, Jr., and Paul Wehr. 1997. *The Persistent Activist: How Peace Commitment Develops and Survives*. Boulder, CO: Westview Press.

Dunne, John Gregory. 1967. *Delano: The Story of the California Grape Strike*. New York: Farrar, Straus, and Giroux.

Ebaugh, Helen Rose Fuchs. 1988. *Becoming an Ex: The Process of Role Exit*. Chicago: University of Chicago Press.

Ellison, Christopher G., and Darren E. Sherkat. 1993. "Conservative Protestantism and Support for Corporal Punishment." *American Sociological Review* 58:131–44.

Fantasia, Rick. 1988. *Cultures of Solidarity: Consciousness, Action, and Contemporary American Workers*. Berkeley: University of California Press.

Fendrich, James Max. 1993. *Ideal Citizens: The Legacy of the Civil Rights Movement*. Albany: State University of New York Press.

Fine, Gary Allan, and Randy Stoecker. 1985. "Can the Circle Be Unbroken: Small Groups and Social Movements." *Advances in Group Processes* 2:1–28.

Freeman, Jo. 1975. *The Politics of Women's Liberation*. New York: David McKay.

Gamson, William. 1990. *The Strategy of Social Protest*. Belmont, CA: Wadsworth.

———. 1991. "Commitment and Agency in Social Movements." *Sociological Forum* 6:27–50.

Ganz, Marshall. 2009. *Why David Sometimes Wins: Leadership, Organization, and Strategy in the California Farm Worker Movement*. New York: Oxford University Press.

Gecas, Viktor. 2000. "Value Identities, Self Motives, and Social Movements." In *Self, Identity, and Social Movements*, edited by S. Stryker, T. J. Owens, and R. W. White, 93–109. Minneapolis: University of Minnesota Press.

Ginsburg, Faye D. 1998. *Contested Lives: The Abortion Debate in an American Community*. Berkeley: University of California Press.

Giugni, Marco G. 2004. "Personal and Biographical Consequences." In *The Blackwell Companion to Social Movements*, edited by David A. Snow, Sarah A. Soule, and H. Kriesi, 489–507. Malden, MA: Blackwell.

Glaser, Barney G., and Anselm L. Strauss. 1967. *The Discovery of Grounded Theory: Strategies for Qualitative Research*. Chicago: Aldine.

Goffman, Erving. 1952. "On Cooling the Mark Out: Some Aspects of Adaptation and Failure." *Psychiatry: Journal of the Study of Interpersonal Relations* 15(4): 451–63.

Gould, Roger V. 1990. "Social Structure and Insurgency in the Paris Commune, 1871." PhD dissertation, Harvard University.

———. 2004. "Why Do Networks Matter? Rationalist and Structuralist Interpretations." In *Social Movements and Networks: Relational Approaches to Collective Action,* edited by Mario Diani and Doug McAdam, 233–57. Oxford: Oxford University Press.

Greenberg, Anna. 2000. "The Church and the Revitalization of Politics and Community." *Political Science Quarterly* 115(3): 377–94.

Hallett, Tim, and Marc J. Ventresca. 2006. "Inhabited Institutions: Social Interactions and Organizational Forms in Gouldner's Patterns of Industrial Bureaucracy." *Theory and Society* 35(2): 213–36.

Heskin, Allan David. 1983. *Tenants and the American Dream: Ideology and the Tenant Movement.* New York: Praeger.

Hirsch, Eric L. 1990. "Sacrifice for the Cause: Group Processes, Recruitment, and Commitment in a Student Social Movement." *American Sociological Review* 55: 243–54.

Hirschman, A. O. 1970. *Exit, Voice, and Loyalty: Responses to Decline in Firms, Organizations, and States.* Cambridge, MA: Harvard University Press.

Honaker, James, Gary King, and Matthew Blackwell. Version 1.2-15. Amelia program. Gking.harvard.edu/Amelia.

Inglehart, Ronald. 1997. *Modernization and Postmodernization: Cultural, Economic and Political Change in 43 Nations.* Princeton, NJ: Princeton University Press.

Jasper, James M. 1998. "The Emotions of Protest: Affective and Reactive Emotions in and around Social Movements." *Sociological Forum* 13:397–424.

Jennings, M. Kent. 1987. "Residues of a Movement: The Aging of the American Protest Generation." *American Political Science Review* 81:365–82.

———. 2002. "Generational Units and the Student Protest Movement in the United States: An Intra- and Intergenerational Analysis." *Political Psychology* 23(2):303–24.

———. 2007. Student–Parent Socialization Study, 1965 [computer file]. Conducted by M. Kent Jennings, University of California. ICPSR07286-v3. Ann Arbor: Inter-university Consortium for Political and Social Research [producer and distributor]. doi:10.3886/ICPSR07286.

Jennings, M. Kent, Gregory B. Markus, and Richard G. Niemi. 1983. Youth–Parent Socialization Panel Study, 1965–1982: Three Waves Combined [computer file]. Ann Arbor: University of Michigan, Center for Political Studies/Survey Research Center [producers]. Ann Arbor: Inter-university Consortium for Political and Social Research [distributor]. doi:10.3886/ICPSR09553.

Jennings, M. Kent, and Richard G. Niemi. 1991. Youth–Parent Socialization Panel Study, 1965–1973 [computer file]. Conducted by University of Michigan, Center for Political Studies. 2nd ICPSR ed. Ann Arbor: Inter-university Consortium for Political and Social Research [producer and distributor]. doi:10.3886/ICPSR07779.

———. 1981. *Generations and Politics: A Panel Study of Young Adults and Their Parents*. Princeton, NJ: Princeton University Press.

Jennings, M. Kent, and Laura Stoker. 2004. Youth–Parent Socialization Panel Study, 1965–1997: Youth Wave IV, 1997. Ann Arbor: University of Michigan.

———. 2005. Youth–Parent Socialization Panel Study, 1965–1997: Youth Wave IV, 1997 [computer file]. ICPSR04023-v2. Ann Arbor: University of Michigan, Center for Political Studies/Survey Research Center [producer]. Ann Arbor: Interuniversity Consortium for Political and Social Research [distributor]. doi:10.3886/ICPSR04023.

Johnson, Jeffrey C. 1990. *Selecting Ethnographic Informants*. Newbury Park, CA: Sage.

Kanter, Rosabeth Moss. 1968. "Commitment and Social Organization: Study of Commitment Mechanisms in Utopian Communities." *American Sociological Review* 33:499–517.

King, Gary, Robert O. Keohane, and Sidney Verba. 1994. *Designing Social Inquiry: Scientific Inference in Qualitative Research*. Princeton, NJ: Princeton University Press.

Kitts, James A. 2000. "Mobilization in Black Boxes: Social Networks and Participation in Social Movement Organizations." *Mobilization* 5(2): 241–57.

Klandermans, Bert. 1984. "Mobilization and Participation: Social Psychological Expansions of Resource Mobilization Theory." *American Sociological Review* 49:583–600.

———. 1997. *The Social Psychology of Protest*. Oxford: Blackwell.

Klandermans, Bert, and Marga de Weerd. 2000. "Group Identification and Political Protest." In *Self, Identity, and Social Movements*, edited by S. Stryker, Timothy J. Owens, and Robert W. White, 68–90. Minneapolis: University of Minnesota Press.

Klandermans, Bert, and Dirk Oegema. 1987. "Potentials, Networks, Motivations and Barriers: Steps towards Participation in Social Movements." *American Sociological Review* 52:519–31.

Klandermans, Bert, Jojanneke van der Toorn, and Jacquelien van Stekelenburg. 2008. "Embeddedness and Identity: How Immigrants Turn Grievances into Action." *American Sociological Review* 73(6): 992–1012.

Klatch, Rebecca E. 1999. *A Generation Divided: The New Left, the New Right, and the 1960s*. Berkeley: University of California Press.

Knoke, David. 1981. "Commitment and Detachment in Voluntary Associations." *American Sociological Review* 46:141–58.

Kubal, T. J. 1998. "The Presentation of Political Self: Cultural Resonance and the Construction of Collective Action Frames." *Sociological Quarterly* 39:539–54.

Larson, Jeff A., and Sarah A. Soule. 2009. "Sector-Level Dynamics and Collective Action in the United States, 1965–1975." *Mobilization* 14(3): 293–314.

Lee, Aie-Rie. 1997. "Exploration of the Sources of Student Activism: The Case of South Korea." *International Journal of Public Opinion Research* 9:48–65.

Leighley, Jan E., and Jonathan Nagler. 1992. "Socioeconomic Class Bias in Turnout, 1964–1988: The Voters Remain the Same." *American Political Science Review* 86: 725–36.

Levy, Jacques. 1975. *Cesar Chavez: An Autobiography of La Causa.* New York: Norton.

Lichterman, Paul. 2005. *Elusive Togetherness: Church Groups Trying to Bridge America's Divisions.* Princeton, NJ: Princeton University Press.

Lofland, John. 1996. *Social Movement Organizations: Guide to Research on Insurgent Realities.* New York: Aldine de Gruyter.

Lofland, John, and Michael Jamison. 1984. "Social Movement Locals: Modal Member Structures." *Sociological Analysis* 45:115–29.

London, Joan, and Henry P. Anderson. 1970. *So Shall Ye Reap.* New York: Crowell.

Luker, Kristin. 1984. *Abortion and the Politics of Motherhood.* Berkeley: University of California Press.

Markus, Gregory B. 1986. "Stability and Change in Political Attitudes: Observed, Recalled, and 'Explained.'" *Political Behavior* 8:21–44.

Marshall, Gordon. 1998. *A Dictionary of Sociology.* Oxford: Oxford University Press.

Martinez, Lisa M. 2005. "Yes We Can: Latino Participation in Unconventional Politics." *Social Forces* 84(1): 135–55.

———. 2008. "The Individual and Contextual Determinants of Protest among Latinos." *Mobilization* 13(2): 189–204.

Marwell, Gerald, Pamela E. Oliver, and Ralph Prahl. 1988. "Social Networks and Collective Action: A Theory of the Critical Mass." *American Journal of Sociology* 94:502–34.

Matthiessen, Anthony. 1969. *Sal Si Puedes: Cesar Chavez and the New American Revolution.* New York: Random House.

McAdam, Doug. 1986. "Recruitment to High-Risk Activism: The Case of Freedom Summer." *American Journal of Sociology* 92:64–90.

———. 1988. *Freedom Summer.* New York: Oxford University Press.

———. 1989. "The Biographical Consequences of Activism." *American Sociological Review* 54:744–60.

———. 1992. "Gender as a Mediator of the Activist Experience: The Case of Freedom Summer." *American Journal of Sociology* 97:1211–40.

———. 1999. *Political Process and the Development of Black Insurgency, 1930–1970.* Chicago: University of Chicago Press.

McAdam, Doug, and Ronnelle Paulsen. 1993. "Specifying the Relationship between Social Ties and Activism." *American Journal of Sociology* 99:640–67.

McCarthy, John D., and Mayer N. Zald. 1973. *The Trend of Social Movements in America: Professionalization and Resource Mobilization*. Morristown, NJ: General Learning Press.

———. 1977. "Resource Mobilization and Social Movements: A Partial Theory." *American Journal of Sociology* 82:1212–41.

McDonald, Katrina Bell. 1997. "Black Activist Mothering." *Gender and Society* 11(6): 773–95.

McPhail, Clark, David Schweingruber, and John McCarthy. 1998. "Policing Protest in the United States: 1960–1995." In *Policing Protest: The Control of Mass Demonstrations in Western Democracies*, edited by Donatella della Porta and Herbert Reiter, 49–69. Minneapolis: University of Minnesota Press.

McPherson, J. Miller. 1977. "Correlates of Social Participation: Comparison of Ethnic Community and Compensatory Theories." *Sociological Quarterly* 18:197–208.

McPherson, J. Miller, Pamela A. Popielarz, and Sonja Drobnič. 1992. "Social Networks and Organizational Dynamics." *American Sociological Review* 57:153–70.

Melucci, Alberto. 1995. "The Process of Collective Identity." In *Social Movements and Culture*, edited by Hank Johnson and Bert Klandermans, 41–63. Minneapolis: University of Minnesota Press.

Melucci, Alberto, John Keane, and Paul Mier. 1989. *Nomads of the Present: Social Movements and Individual Needs in Contemporary Society*. Philadelphia: Temple University Press.

Meyer, David S., and Sidney Tarrow, eds. 1998. *The Social Movement Society: Contentious Politics for a New Century*. Lanham, MD: Rowman and Littlefield.

Meyer, David S., and Nancy Whittier. 1994. "Social Movement Spillover." *Social Problems* 41:277–98.

Moen, Matthew C. 1992. *The Transformation of the Christian Right*. Tuscaloosa: University of Alabama Press.

Morris, Aldon. 1981. "Black Southern Student Sit-In Movement: An Analysis of Internal Organization." *American Sociological Review* 46:744–67.

Muller, Edward N., and Thomas O. Jukam. 1977. "The Meaning of Political Support." *American Political Science Review* 71:1561–95.

Neitz, Mary Jo. 1987. *Charisma and Community: A Study of Religious Commitment within the Charismatic Renewal*. New Brunswick, NJ: Transaction.

Nepstad, Sharon Erickson. 2004. "Persistent Resistance: Commitment and Community in the Plowshares Movement." *Social Problems* 51:43–60.

Nepstad, Sharon Erickson, and Christian Smith. 1999. "Rethinking Recruitment to High-Risk/Cost Activism: The Case of the Nicaragua Exchange." *Mobilization* 4:25–40.

Norris, Pippa. 2002. *Democratic Phoenix: Reinventing Political Activism*. Cambridge: Cambridge University Press.

Nuttbrock, Larry, and Patricia Freudiger. 1991. "Identity Theory and Motherhood: A Test of Stryker's Theory." *Social Psychology Quarterly* 54:146–57.

Oegema, Dirk, and Bert Klandermans. 1994. "Why Social Movement Sympathizers Don't Participate: Erosion and Nonconversion of Support." *American Sociological Review* 59(5): 703–22.

Okamoto, Dina. 2003. "Towards a Theory of Panethnicity: Explaining Asian American Collective Action." *American Sociological Review* 68(6): 811–42.

Oliver, Pamela. 1984. "If You Don't Do It, Nobody Else Will: Active and Token Contributors to Local Collective Action." *American Sociological Review* 49:601–10.

Olsen, Marvin Elliott. 1970. "Social and Political Participation of Blacks." *American Sociological Review* 35:682–97.

Opp, Karl-Dieter, and Christiane Gern. 1993. "Dissident Groups, Personal Networks, and Spontaneous Cooperation: The East-German Revolution of 1989." *American Sociological Review* 58:659–80.

Page, Ann L., and Donald A. Clelland. 1978. "Kanawha County Textbook Controversy: A Study of the Politics of Life Style Concern." *Social Forces* 57:265–81.

Passy, Florence, and Marco Giugni. 2000. "Life-Spheres, Networks, and Sustained Participation in Social Movements: A Phenomenological Approach to Political Commitment." *Sociological Forum* 15:117–44.

———. 2001. "Social Networks and Individual Perceptions: Explaining Differential Participation in Social Movements." *Sociological Forum* 16:123–53.

Peteet, Julie. 1997. "Icons and Militants: Mothering in the Danger Zone." *Signs* 23(1): 103–29.

Piehl, Mel. 1982. *Breaking the Bread: The Catholic Worker and the Origin of Catholic Radicalism in America*. Philadelphia: Temple University Press.

Polletta, Francesca, and James M. Jasper. 2001. "Collective Identity and Social Movements." *Annual Review of Sociology* 27:283–305.

Putnam, Robert D. 2000. *Bowling Alone: The Collapse and Revival of American Community*. New York: Simon and Schuster.

Rochford, E. Burke. 1985. *Hare Krishna in America*. New Brunswick, NJ: Rutgers University Press.

Rogers, Everett M. 1983. *Diffusion of Innovations*. New York: Free Press.

Rohlinger, Deana A. 2002. "Framing the Abortion Debate: Organizational Resources, Media Strategies, and Movement-Countermovement Dynamics." *Sociological Quarterly* 43:479–507.

Rosenstone, Steven J., and John Mark Hansen. 1993. *Mobilization, Participation, and Democracy in America*. New York: Macmillan.

Rosenthal, Naomi, and Michael Schwartz. 1989. "Spontaneity and Democracy in Social Protest." *International Social Movement Research* 13:33–60.

Rubin, Donald B. 1987. *Multiple Imputation for Nonresponse in Surveys*. New York: Wiley.

Rupp, L. J., and V. A. Taylor. 1987. *Survival in the Doldrums: The American Women's Rights Movement, 1945 to the 1960s.* New York: Oxford University Press.

Sandell, Rickard. 1999. "Organizational Life aboard the Moving Bandwagons: A Network Analysis of Dropouts from a Swedish Temperance Organization, 1896–1937." *Acta Sociologica* 42:3–15.

Schacter, Daniel L. 1996. *Searching for Memory: The Brain, the Mind, and the Past.* New York: Basic Books.

Schreiber, Ronnee. 2002. "Injecting a Woman's Voice: Conservative Women's Organizations, Gender Consciousness, and the Expression of Women's Policy Preferences." *Sex Roles* 47:331–42.

Scott, Jacqueline, and Duane Alwin. 1998. "Retrospective versus Prospective Measurement of Life Histories in Longitudinal Research." In *Methods of Life Course Research: Qualitative and Quantitative Approaches,* edited by G. Elder Jr. and J. Ziele, 98–127. Thousand Oaks, CA: Sage.

Sherkat, Darren E., and T. Jean Blocker. 1993. "Environmental Activism in the Protest Generation: Differentiating 1960s Activists." *Youth & Society* 25:140–61.

Smith, Christian. 1991. *The Emergence of Liberation Theology: Radical Religion and Social Movement Theory.* Chicago: University of Chicago Press.

Snow, David A. 2001. "Collective Identity and Expressive Forms." Center for the Study of Democracy Working Paper Series. Irvine, CA. http:/scholarship.org/us/item/2zn1t7bj.

Snow, David A., and Leon Anderson. 1993. *Down on Their Luck: A Study of Homeless Street People.* Berkeley: University of California Press.

Snow, David A., and Robert D. Benford. 1992. "Master Frames and Cycles of Protest." In *Frontiers in Social Movement Theory,* edited by A. D. Morris and C. M. Mueller, 133–55. New Haven, CT: Yale University Press.

Snow, David A., and Pamela E. Oliver. 1993. "Social Movements and Collective Behavior: Social Psychological Dimensions and Considerations." In *Sociological Perspectives on Social Psychology,* edited by Karen Cook, Gary Allen Fine, and James House, 571–99. Needham Heights, MA: Allyn and Bacon.

Snow, David A., and Cynthia L. Phillips. 1980. "The Lofland-Stark Conversion Model: A Critical Reassessment." *Social Problems* 27:430–47.

Snow, David A., Steven K. Worden, E. Burke Rochford, and Robert D. Benford. 1986. "Frame Alignment Processes, Micromobilization, and Movement Participation." *American Sociological Review* 51:464–81.

Snow, David A., Leon A. Zurcher, and Sheldon Ekland-Olson. 1980. "Social Networks and Social Movements: A Microstructural Approach to Differential Recruitment." *American Sociological Review* 45:787–801.

Staggenborg, Suzanne. 1987. "Life-Style Preferences and Social Movement Recruitment: Illustrations for the Abortion Conflict." *Social Science Quarterly* 68(4): 779–97.

Steers, Richard M. 1977. "Antecedents and Outcomes of Organizational Commitment." *Administrative Science Quarterly* 22:46–56.

Stekelenburg, Jacquelien van, and Bert Klandermans. 2007. "Individuals in Movements." In *Handbook of Social Movements across Disciplines*, edited by B. Klandermans and C. Roggeband, 157–204. New York: Springer.

Stoker, Laura, and M. Kent Jennings. 1995. "Life-Cycle Transitions and Political Participation: The Case of Marriage." *American Political Science Review* 89(2): 421–33.

Stryker, Sheldon. 1980. *Symbolic Interactionism: A Social Structural Version.* Menlo Park, CA: Benjamin Cummings.

Stryker, Sheldon, and Richard T. Serpe. 1994. "Identity Salience and Psychological Centrality: Equivalent, Overlapping, or Complementary Concepts." *Social Psychology Quarterly* 57:16–35.

Tarrow, Sidney. 1996. "Social Movements in Contentious Politics." *American Political Science Review* 90(4): 874–83.

Taylor, Verta. 1989. "Social Movement Continuity: The Women's Movement in Abeyance." *American Sociological Review* 54:761–75.

Taylor, Verta, and N. C. Raeburn. 1995. "Identity Politics as High-Risk Activism: Career Consequences for Lesbian, Gay, and Bisexual Sociologists." *Social Problems* 42(2): 252–73.

Taylor, Verta, and Nancy E. Whittier. 1995. "Analytical Approaches to Social Movement Culture: The Culture of the Women's Movement." In *Social Movements and Culture*, edited by Hank Johnston and Bert Klandermans, 163–87. Minneapolis: University of Minnesota Press.

Teixeira, Ruy A. 1992. *The Disappearing American Voter.* Washington, DC: Brookings Institution.

Teske, Nathan. 1997. *Political Activists in America: The Identity Construction Model of Political Participation.* Cambridge: Cambridge University Press.

Thorne, Barrie. 1975. "Women in the Draft Resistance Movement: Case Study of Sex Roles and Social Movements." *Sex Roles* 1(2): 179–95.

Tilly, Charles. 2005. *Identities, Boundaries, and Social Ties.* Boulder, CO: Paradigm Publishers.

Toch, Hans. 1965. *The Social Psychology of Social Movements.* Indianapolis: Bobbs-Merrill.

United States Census Bureau. 1960. http://www2.census.gov/prod2/statcomp/documents/1965-01.pdf.

Useem, Bert. 1998. "Breakdown Theories of Collective Action." *Annual Review of Sociology* 24:215–38.

Vall, Mark van de. 1963. *De vakbeweging in een welvaartsstaat.* Meppel, Netherlands: Bobbs-Merrill.

Veen, Gerrita van der, and Bert Klandermans. 1989. "'Exit' Behavior in Social Movement Organizations." *International Social Movement Research* 2:179–98.

Verba, Sidney, Kay Lehman Schlozman, and Henry E. Brady. 1995. *Voice and Equality: Civic Voluntarism in American Politics*. Cambridge, MA: Harvard University Press.

Warren, Mark. 1990. "Ideology and the Self." *Theory and Society* 19:599–634.

———. 2001. *Democracy and Association*. Princeton, NJ: Princeton University Press.

Weiss, Robert F. 1963. "Defection from Social Movements and Subsequent Recruitment to New Movements." *Sociometry* 26:1–20.

Whalen, Jack, and Richard Flacks. 1989. *Beyond the Barricades: The Sixties Generation Grows Up*. Philadelphia: Temple University Press.

Whittier, Nancy. 1995. *Feminist Generations: The Persistence of the Radical Women's Movement*. Philadelphia: Temple University Press.

Wiltfang, Gregory L., and Doug McAdam. 1991. "The Costs and Risks of Social Activism: A Study of Sanctuary Movement Activism." *Social Forces* 69(4): 987–1010.

Wolch, Jennifer R., and Michael J. Dear. 1993. *Malign Neglect: Homelessness in an American City*. San Francisco: Jossey-Bass.

Wong, Janelle S. 2005. "Mobilizing Asian-American Voters: A Field Experiment." *Annals of the American Academy of Political and Social Sciences* 601:102–14.

Wooldridge, Jeffrey M. 2001. *Econometric Analysis of Cross Section and Panel Data*. Cambridge, MA: MIT Press.

Wright, Charles R., and Herbert H. Hyman. 1958. "Voluntary Association Memberships of American Adults: Evidence from National Sample Surveys." *American Sociological Review* 23:284–94.

Xu, Jun. 2005. "Why Do Minorities Participate Less? The Effects of Immigration, Education, and Electoral Process on Asian American Voter Registration and Turnout." *Social Science Research* 34(4): 682–702.

Zald, Mayer N., and John D. McCarthy. 1987. "Social Movement Industries: Competition and Conflict among SMOs." In *Social Movements in an Organizational Society*, edited by Mayer Zald and John McCarthy, 161–80. New Brunswick, NJ: Transaction.

Index

Italic page numbers indicate material in tables or figures.